Lecture Notes in Computer Science   9997

Commenced Publication in 1973
Founding and Former Series Editors:
Gerhard Goos, Juris Hartmanis, and Jan van Leeuwen

More information about this series at http://www.springer.com/series/7412

Mohamed Chetouani · Jeffrey Cohn
Albert Ali Salah (Eds.)

Human Behavior Understanding

7th International Workshop, HBU 2016
Amsterdam, The Netherlands, October 16, 2016
Proceedings

 Springer

Editors
Mohamed Chetouani
Université Pierre et Marie Curie
Paris
France

Jeffrey Cohn
University of Pittsburgh
Pittsburgh, PA
USA

Albert Ali Salah
Bogazici University
Bebek, Istanbul
Turkey

ISSN 0302-9743 ISSN 1611-3349 (electronic)
Lecture Notes in Computer Science
ISBN 978-3-319-46842-6 ISBN 978-3-319-46843-3 (eBook)
DOI 10.1007/978-3-319-46843-3

Library of Congress Control Number: 2016952516

LNCS Sublibrary: SL6 – Image Processing, Computer Vision, Pattern Recognition, and Graphics

Printed on acid-free paper

This Springer imprint is published by Springer Nature
The registered company is Springer International Publishing AG
The registered company address is: Gewerbestrasse 11, 6330 Cham, Switzerland

Preface

The HBU workshops gather researchers dealing with the problem of modeling human behavior under its multiple facets (expression of emotions, display of complex social and relational behaviors, performance of individual or joint actions, etc.). This year, the seventh edition of the workshop was organized with challenges of designing solutions with children in mind, with the cross-pollination of different disciplines, bringing together researchers of multimedia, robotics, HCI, artificial intelligence, pattern recognition, interaction design, ambient intelligence, and psychology. The diversity of human behavior, the richness of multi-modal data that arises from its analysis, and the multitude of applications that demand rapid progress in this area ensure that the HBU workshops provide a timely and relevant discussion and dissemination platform.

The HBU workshops were previously organized as satellite events to the ICPR (Istanbul, Turkey, 2010), AMI (Amsterdam, The Netherlands, 2011), IROS (Vilamoura, Portugal, 2012), ACM Multimedia (Barcelona, Spain, 2013), ECCV (Zurich, Switzerland, 2014) and UBICOMP (Osaka, Japan, 2015) conferences, with different focus themes. The focus theme of this year's HBU workshop was "Behavior Analysis and Multimedia for Children."

With each passing year, children begin using computers and related devices at younger and younger ages. The initial age of computer usage is steadily getting lower, yet there are many open issues in children's use of computers and multimedia. In order to tailor multimedia applications to children, we need smarter applications that understand and respond to the users' behavior, distinguishing children and adults if necessary. Collecting data from children and working with children in interactive applications call for additional skills and interdisciplinary collaborations. Subsequently, this year's workshop promoted research on the automatic analysis of children's behavior. Specifically, the call for papers solicited contributions on age estimation, detection of abusive and aggressive behaviors, cyberbullying, inappropriate content detection, privacy and ethics of multimedia access for children, databases collected from children, monitoring children during social interactions, and investigations into children's interaction with multimedia content.

The keynote speakers of the workshop were Dr. Paul Vogt (Tilburg University), with a talk entitled "Modelling Child Language Acquisition in Interaction from Corpora" and Dr. Isabela Granic (Radboud University Nijmegen), with a talk on "Bridging Developmental Science and Game Design to Video Games That Build Emotional Resilience." We thank our keynotes for their contributions.

This proceedings volume contains the papers presented at the workshop. We received 17 submissions, of which 10 were accepted for oral presentation at the workshop (the acceptance rate is 58 %). Each paper was reviewed by at least two members of the Technical Program Committee. The papers submitted by the co-chairs were handled by other chairs both during reviewing and during decisions. The Easy-Chair system was used for processing the papers. The present volume collects the accepted papers, revised for the proceedings in accordance with reviewer comments, and presented at the workshop. The papers are organized into thematic sections on "Behavior Analysis During Play," "Daily Behaviors," "Vision-Based Applications," and "Gesture and Movement Analysis." Together with the invited talks, the focus theme was covered in one paper session as well as in a panel session organized by Dr. Rita Cucchiara (University of Modena and Reggio Emilia).

We would like to take the opportunity to thank our Program Committee members and reviewers for their rigorous feedback as well as our authors and our invited speakers for their contributions.

October 2016

Mohamed Chetouani
Jeffrey Cohn
Albert Ali Salah

Organization

Conference Co-chairs

Mohamed Chetouani	Université Pierre et Marie Curie, France
Jeffrey Cohn	Carnegie Mellon University and University of Pittsburgh, USA
Albert Ali Salah	Boğaziçi University, Turkey

Technical Program Committee

Elisabeth André	Universität Augsburg, Germany
Lisa Anthony	University of Florida, USA
Oya Aran	Idiap Research Institute, Switzerland
Antonio Camurri	University of Genoa, Italy
Marco Cristani	University of Verona, Italy
Abhinav Dhall	University of Canberra, Australia
Hamdi Dibeklioğlu	Delft University of Technology, The Netherlands
Weidong Geng	Zhejiang University, China
Hatice Gunes	University of Cambridge, UK
Sibel Halfon	Bilgi University, Turkey
Zakia Hammal	Carnegie Mellon University, USA
Dirk Heylen	University of Twente, The Netherlands
Andri Ioannou	Cyprus University of Technology, Cyprus
Mohan Kankanhalli	National University of Singapore, Singapore
Alexey Karpov	SPIIRAS, Russia
Heysem Kaya	Namık Kemal University, Turkey
Cem Keskin	Microsoft Research, USA
Hatice Kose	Istanbul Technical University, Turkey
Ben Kröse	University of Amsterdam, The Netherlands
Matei Mancas	University of Mons, Belgium
Panos Markopoulos	Eindhoven University of Technology, The Netherlands
Louis-Philippe Morency	Carnegie Mellon University, USA
Florian Mueller	RMIT, Australia
Helio Pedrini	University of Campinas, Brazil
Francisco Florez Revuelta	Kingston University, UK
Stefan Scherer	University of Southern California, USA
Ben Schouten	Eindhoven University of Technology, The Netherlands
Suleman Shahid	University of Tilburg, The Netherlands
Reiner Wichert	AHS Assisted Home Solutions, Germany
Bian Yang	Norwegian University of Science and Technology, Norway

Additional Reviewers

Necati Cihan Camgöz
Irtiza Hasan
Giorgio Roffo
Ahmet Alp Kındıroğlu

Contents

Vision Based Applications

Behavior Analysis During Play

EmoGame: Towards a Self-Rewarding Methodology for Capturing Children Faces in an Engaging Context

Benjamin Allaert[(✉)], José Mennesson, and Ioan Marius Bilasco

Univ. Lille, CNRS, Central Lille, UMR 9189 - CRIStAL - Centre de Recherche
en Informatique Signal et Automatique de Lille, 59000 Lille, France
benjamin.allaert@ed.univ-lille1.fr,
{jose.mennesson,marius.bilasco}@univ-lille1.fr

Abstract. Facial expression datasets are currently limited as most of them only capture the emotional expressions of adults. Researchers have begun to assert the importance of having child exemplars of the various emotional expressions in order to study the interpretation of these expressions developmentally. Capturing children expression is more complicated as the protocols used for eliciting and recording expressions for adults are not necessarily adequate for children. This paper describes the creation of a flexible Emotional Game for capturing children faces in an engaging context. The game is inspired by the well-known Guitar HeroTM gameplay, but instead of playing notes, the player should produce series of expressions. In the current work, we measure the capacity of the game to engage the children and we discuss the requirements in terms of expression recognition needed to ensure a viable gameplay. The preliminary experiments conducted with a group of 12 children with ages between 7 and 11 in various settings and social contexts show high levels of engagement and positive feedback.

1 Introduction

Facial identity and expression play critical roles in our social lives. Faces are therefore frequently used as stimuli in a variety of areas of scientific research. A great amount of work has been provided for adult face expression recognition. However, the existing state of the art solutions do not generalize well for children faces and for child-related contexts. As most of the existing solutions for expression recognition are data-learning oriented, they strongly depend on the underlying learning corpus. One cause for poor generalization is effectively, the lack of specific children databases. Although several extensive databases of adult faces exist, few databases include child faces. The lack of specific children dataset are due to issues related to image property and privacy, but also, to the protocols and tools used for capturing dataset that are appropriate for adults but not necessarily adequate for children.

In most of the proposed recording scenarios the subjects are passive or are acting on demand, but they are not naturally engaged in the interaction. The elicitation of expression is most of the time explicit. Some of the recent databases

© Springer International Publishing AG 2016
M. Chetouani et al. (Eds.): HBU 2016, LNCS 9997, pp. 3–14, 2016.
DOI: 10.1007/978-3-319-46843-3_1

like SEMAINE [13] or RECOLA [17] are proposing (limited) social interactions: agent to human or human to human. Still, the lab context tends to bias expressions as the subjects are not in their natural environment. In these settings, the vivid/spontaneous expressions are captured in between recording sessions, when the subjects are interacting with the lab personnel. On the other hand, capturing databases in natural environments is challenging as the position of microphones and cameras is not fully controlled, there is noise like visual backgrounds and it is difficult to control the emotional content eliciting expressions.

Participating to recording session is not perceived as an enjoying task. Usually people are rewarded explicitly in order to participate to the recordings. We think, that especially for children, the reward should be implicit as subject should enjoy the session. We propose an interactive and non-intrusive tool for capturing children faces in an engaging context. We provide an emo-related game, inspired by the well known Guitar HeroTM game, where children have to produce expressions in order to score points. The application was ported on portable devices (tablet, smartphone) so that it can be easily deployed in-the-wild environments. The engaging scenario ensures control over the capturing conditions. While playing, the subjects become aware that without visual contact, in poor lighting condition, in absence of frontal faces they acquire little or no points. In preliminary experiments, we observed that they strive to conform to the technology limitation in order to score as much points as possible. Viable sessions (frontal poses, good lighting, etc.) can be distinguish from poor ones by the scores acquired.

While the children are using the application, we expect to collect data that is partially annotated, as subjects in good mental health, will strive to produce the required emotion at expected moments in time. Most of the time the expressions are expected to be acted and exaggerated in order to acquire more points. But sill, vivid and spontaneous expressions can be elicited when the gameplay is tuned. High speed variations in emotions sequence generally produce natural hilarity, especially when the game is played in a social context with friends. Defective expression recognition tends to induce spontaneous negative expressions. With regard to the current databases, which generally provides a neutral-onset-apex-offset schema, the proposed solution allows to obtain more complex patterns, including fading from one emotion to another.

The preliminary experiments conducted with a group of 12 children with ages between 7 and 11 in various settings and social contexts (home - alone or with friends or family, school, work) show the rapid adoption of the application and the high engagement and enjoyment of the subjects in participating to the recording session. Due to privacy and image property, at this stage, no visual data was collected. The recording sessions were conducted in order to measure the adequacy of the developed tool and protocol for capturing child expression in various contexts and in an enjoying way.

The paper is structured as follows. First, we discuss existing methodologies for capturing expression-related databases. Then, we discuss methodologies and scenarios aiming to increase the attractiveness of recording sessions. An application reflecting the proposed methodology is presented, as well as the time-efficient expression recognition technologies. We report on the preliminary results obtained for recording sessions concerning children and young adults. Finally, conclusions and perspectives are discussed.

2   Related Works

Motivated by a wide range of applications, researchers in computer vision and pattern recognition have become increasingly interested in developing algorithms for automatic expressions recognition in still images and videos. Most of the existing solutions are data-driven and large quantities of data are required to train classifiers. Three main types of interaction scenarios have been used to record emotionally colored interactions, most of the time for adults:

- **Acted behavior** presented in CK+ [10] and ADFES [23] database is produced by the subject upon request, e.g., actors. Interaction scenarios with a static pose and acted behavior are the easiest to design and present the advantage to have a control on the portrayed emotions. However, this approach was criticized for including (non-realistic) forced traits of emotion, which are claimed to be much more subtle when the emotion arises in a real-life context [19].
- **Induced behavior** occurs in a controlled setting designed to elicit an emotional reaction such as when watching movies like in DISFA [2]. Active scenarios based on the induced behavior can influence on subject behavior with indirect control of the behaviors of participants, by imposing a specific context of interaction, e.g., four emotionally stereotyped conversational agents were used in SEMAINE database [13]. However, this approach may not provide fully natural behaviors, because the interaction may be restricted to a specific context, wherein the spontaneous aspect of interaction may be thus limited or even absent [21].
- **Spontaneous behavior** appears in social settings such as interactions between humans as in RECOLA database [17]. The spontaneous behavior scenario guarantees natural emotionally colored interactions, since the set of verbal and non-verbal cues is both free and unlimited. However, this spontaneous interaction scenario is the hardest to design as it includes several ethical issues, like people discussing about private things, or not knowing they are recorded.

The above scenarios were successfully employed in collecting adult databases [2,10,13,17,23]. Child databases are needed to train solution tuned for child expression analysis. Recently, child databases are becoming available [4,7,15]. The databases are generally created under the protocols used for capturing adult databases and more specifically using the acted and induced behavior protocols.

The Dartmouth Database of Children's Faces [4] is a well-controlled database of faces of 40 males and 40 females children between 6 and 16 years-of-age. Eight different facial expressions are imitated by each model. During acquisition, children were seated front of a black screen and were dressed in black. In order to elicit the desired facial expressions, models were asked to imagine situations (e.g. Disgust: "Imagine you are covered with chewing gum", or, Anger: "Imagine your brother or sister broke your PlayStation"), and photos were taken when the expressions were the best the children could produce.

The most extensive children databases is the NIMH Child Emotional Faces Picture Set (NIMH-ChEFS) [7], which includes frontal face images of 60 children between 10 and 17 years-of-age, posing five facial expressions. Each child actor was instructed to act a specific facial emotion. The dataset includes children of different races, multiple facial expressions and gaze orientations.

EmoWinconsin [15] recorded children between 7 and 13 years old while playing a card game with an adult examiner. The game is based on a neuropsychological test, modified to encourage dialogue and induce emotions in the player because children are deeply involved in its realization. Each sequence is annotated with six emotional categories and three continuous emotion primitives by 11 human evaluators. The children's performance and interaction with the examiner trigger reactions that affect children's emotional state. Influencing the children's mood during the experiment, by imposing for example a specific context of interaction (positive and negative sessions), may thus be useful to ensure a variety of behaviors during the interactions.

By analyzing the protocols that have been used to elaborate the children databases, we believe that more natural interactions, with limited technology constraints shall be provided in order to increase the children engagement and collect more vivid expressions. Although there are not many databases of children with annotated facial expressions available, games are being used more and more to eliciting emotions. The games provide a useful tool for capturing children faces, while imposing a specific context (social environment, interaction). In [20] Shahid et al. explore the effect of physical co-presence on the emotional expressions of game playing children. They showed that the emotional response of children varies when they play a game alone or together with their friends. Indeed, children in pairs are more expressive than individuals because they have been influenced by their partners.

Motivated by the interest of children in games, we propose a methodology and a tool for capturing interactive and non-intrusive emo-related expressions. It is important to specify that our tool does not retain personal data and, in its current state, it does not record facial images. The goal is to evaluate the impact of a new protocol that encourages children to produce facial expressions under close to in-the-wild conditions. As illustrated in [15,20], a game seems an appropriate context because children are strongly involved and they become more collaborative. Moreover, a mobile support allows the recordings outside a (living) lab context, hence, children can be recorded in an unbiased fashion in more natural circumstances (in a spirit of a family home, friendship). While conducted in a social context, the pilot is expected to capture vivid expressions in between or during the game. The protocol can be tuned in order to induce negative expression like frustration in biasing the behavior of the game. More insights about the design of the game scenario is provided in the next section.

3   Game Scenario

Similar to the Guitar HeroTM gameplay, we ask subjects to produce a series of positive, negative and surprise expressions as illustrated in Fig. 1. The objective of the game is to match facial expression that scroll down the screen and get points depending on the capacity to reproduce it. Successive successfully reproducing of required expressions provides combos producing best scores possible and encouraging the children to keep their attention focused on the interface and produce the good expressions. The application offers the possibility to add additional expressions (Fig. 1(1–7)). In our preliminary study, we are exploring the positive (green column), surprise (blue column) and negative (red column) expressions. We could also adapt the system to consider actions units from Facial Action Coding System (FACS) proposed by Ekman [8].

As illustrated in Fig. 1, the game interface is composed of seven major elements. Each expression is associated with one column and one token with a visual representation of the expression (Fig. 1(1–3) represent a positive expression token) in a particular color. When a token is reaching the bottom circle of the board (Fig. 1(1–4)), the player face (Fig. 1(1–5)) and the expression which should be found are analyzed to assign a grade (Fig. 1(1–1) and keep track of the accumulated score (Fig. 1(1–2)). These individual ratings aggregated provide an overall rating for the game. The gauge above the score indicates the overall rating during the course of the game. As visual facial feedback is provided, when expression

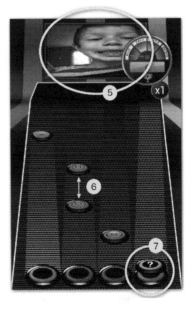

Fig. 1. EmoGame interface inspired to the Guitar Hero^{TM} gameplay. (Color figure online)

recognition fails, the user is implicitly encouraged to control the quality of the image by correcting the orientation and the position, in order to ensure optimal conditions (no backlight, frontal face, homogeneous illumination, etc.)

In order to enhance user engagement and enjoyment we have added textual (perfect, good, fair, bad) and audio (positive or negative) feedback. In order to be able to collect data for longer times, it is important to provide a positive game-playing experience. The game-playing experience is also influenced by the sequence of tokens presented to the user. The sequence of events is fully program-mable and does make a difference in terms of player behavior. The speed of token going down the screen, the time distance between consecutive tokens (Fig. 1(1–6)) and the order of appearance of the token can be customized. In preliminary test-ings, we have observed that high speed variations in emotions sequence generally produce natural hilarity, especially when the game is played in a social context with friends. Besides, the deployed technology for expression recognition must be robust enough in order to keep the child committed to the experience. However, an expression palette larger than the one that the application can recognize can be collected, as long as a minimum set of expressions is recognized and points are coherently scored for the supported expressions.

In the following we focus on the application and on the details of the under-lying methods for positive, negative and surprise expression recognition.

4   Expression Recognition

In the context of a video game, the expression analysis must be performed as fast as possible (in interactive time) in order to keep the attention and involvement of the player. These requirements are even more important when the expression recognition is performed in a mobile context where memory, computational capa-bilities and energy are limited. We propose a fast analysis process in two stages illustrated in Fig. 2: image pre-processing detailed in Sect. 4.1 and expression recognition detailed in Sect. 4.2.

A good technical realization is necessary to keep player attention focused during the session and to ensure that the objectives of the scenario are fulfilled. The Fig. 3 illustrate the process of capturing the facial expressions. Once the token scrolls down and reaches the bottom circles, the image provided by the frontal camera of the hand-held device is extracted and sent through the JNI interface to the expression from face library. The expression analysis is done by the native library and results are sent back to the application controller which updates the score and provides textual and audio feedback to the user.

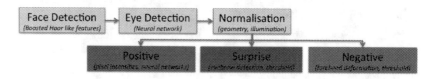

Fig. 2. Overview of the facial expression recognition process

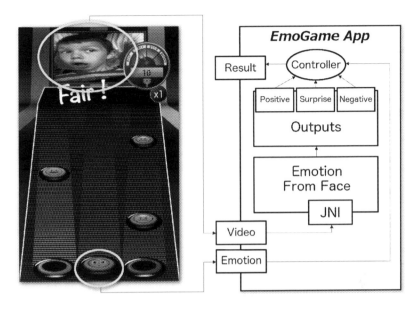

Fig. 3. The EmoGame expression analyzer process. Results are calculated from the metrics estimated on the player face and the required expression.

4.1 Image Pre-processing

As soon as the image is received through the JNI interface, image pre-processing is performed. The goal is to detect the face and make it invariant under translation, rotation, scale and illumination.

As the application is deployed in a hand-held mobile device, most of the time the person face is situated in the center of the image. A fast face detector such as Boosted Haar classifiers [24] is used to localize the face of the user. This kind of classifiers presents some drawbacks since they support only a limited set of near to frontal head-poses. Supposing that the user is engaged in the game, each frame of the video contains a single face. The absence of a face is a sign for either non supported head-poses (e.g. looking somewhere else) or inadequate hand-held device orientation (e.g. camera device pointing above the face).

We use a dedicated neural network defined by Rowley [18] (available in STASM library [14]) in order to detect the eye positions. Orientation of the face is estimated using the vertical positions of the two eyes. The angle between the two pupil points is used to correct the orientation by setting the face center as origin point and the whole frame is rotated in opposite direction. Finally, the face is cropped and its size is normalized to obtain scale invariance. Image intensity is normalized using histogram equalization which improve its contrast. It aims to eliminate light and illumination related defects from the facial area.

4.2   Face Expression Analysis

By normalizing the face representation (invariant under translation, rotation and scale), we can compute fast metrics directly on pixels rather than extracting complex metrics that can have high computational complexity. Positive expression are recognized by considering raw pixel intensities. Negative and surprise expressions are detected by characterizing changes in small regions of interests.

Positive expression detection: In this application, positive expression detection is performed using method defined in [6]. The dataset GENKI-4K [1] is used as a training set for positive/neutral classification. Only the lower part of the normalized face which maximizes the accuracy for this particular classification problem is considered. A back propagation neural network having two hidden layers (20 and 15 neurons) is used to train pixel intensity values obtained from the selected ROI. Input layer has 200 neurons and output layer has two neurons representing the happy and neutral classes. Experiments on positive expression detection are conducted in [6] and state-of-the art performances are obtained on GENKI-4K [1] (92 %), JAFFE [12] (82 %) and FERET [16] (91 %) databases.

Negative expression detection: Negative expressions generally involves the activation of various degrees of FACS AU4 where eyebrows are lowered and drawn together [9]. We focus on the regions of interests located in the upper part of the face which include wrinkles between the eyes. The wrinkles are extracted using a Gabor filters bank as in [3]. Each pixel of the resulting image corresponds to the maximum amplitude among the filtered responses. Then, the resulting image is normalized and thresholded to obtain a binary image. The feature encoding AU4 activation corresponds to the proportion of white pixels, which corresponds to wrinkles. A threshold is used to determine if there is a negative expression or not. To show the role of the threshold, KDEF database [11] is considered to perform tests. In our experiment, negative expressions cover anger, disgust, afraid and sad expression as in [9]. A recall-precision curve obtained by varying the threshold is shown in Fig. 4. It can be easily seen that obtained results are good enough to provide a consistent feedback to the user. In KDEF experiments, a proportion of white pixels superior to 0 % gives the best results in terms of recall-precision as the dataset was captured in control settings and forehead is cleared of artifacts. However, while playing an adaptive threshold has to be employed in order to better support variations due to shadows and camera orientation.

Surprise expression detection: It is well-known that surprise expression is closely related to the activation of FACS AU1 and FACS AU2 [22], which correspond, respectively, to left and right eyebrows movements. In this paper, eyebrows are detected using a Gabor filter applied to a ROI determined experimentally considering the eye position and the IPD distance as in [5]. The feature encoding AU1 or AU2 activation is the ratio between the distance of the eye center and the lower boundary of the eyebrow and the distance between the two eyes. Higher this feature is, more the person raises eyebrows. The surprise expression is detected when this feature is higher then threshold. This feature has been

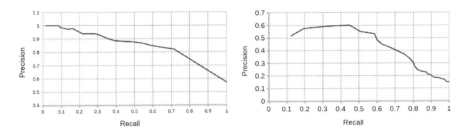

Fig. 4. Recall-Precision curve on KDEF: negative expression detection evaluation (on the left) and negative expression detection evaluation (on the right)

chosen because it is fast to compute and the obtained results are good enough in our context. To test the stability of the feature against the threshold used, an experiment has been conducted on KDEF database [11]. A recall-precision curve obtained by varying the surprise threshold is shown in Fig. 4. In KDEF experiments, a threshold equals to 33 gives the best results in terms of recall-precision. As for the negative expression, while playing, an adaptive threshold has to be employed in order to take into account camera orientation.

5 Preliminary Experiments

In this section, we study the capacity of our application to engage the children in the scenarized recording sessions. Moreover, we want to measure the satisfaction of subjects and their intention to renew the experience.

For the experiments, we used a Samsung Galaxy Tab 2 10.1 digital tablet. The application layout is adapted to the landscape mode as the front camera is situated in the middle of the long side of the tablet.

Each game is composed of 15 expressions to mimic (5 Positive, 5 Negative, 5 Surprise). The sequence of expressions is randomized. The speed of tokens scrolling down is constant but the gap between them varies randomly.

Twelve children and six adults were invited to test the application. We have divided them into three age categories: between 4 and 7 years old, between 8 and 10 years old and adults (> 20 years old). Sessions were recorder either at home or at school, alone or with friends.

Each subject played freely the game once or several times. Then, he filled in a questionnaire measuring the enjoyment, and his intention to play again. We also asked the player about the ability of the application to detect correctly the expressions. Each response is ranged between 1 for bad and 5 for great. The results of this experimentation is shown in Fig. 5.

The perception of the expression recognition performances varies within the children groups (see Fig. 5A). Older children were challenging more the application and were able to identify situations were the technology is failing (high pitch, poor lighting conditions, near field of view). However, we have noted that children were motivated to play again in order to improve their score by correcting

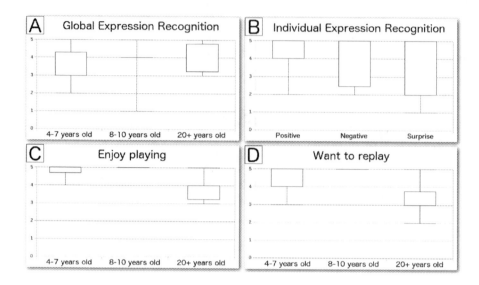

Fig. 5. Boxplots showing several statistics computed on our experiments

device orientation and trying various ways of producing the required expressions. Finally, we can see that for all testers, positive expression seems to be the best detected by our game (see in Fig. 5B). Negative and surprise expression detection results depends strongly on the facial characteristics of the player and illumination settings. In this case, adaptive thresholding could improve results concerning these features. Despite the recognition errors, in Fig. 5C, we can clearly see that all age groups enjoyed the game. Children enjoyed better than adults and were more committed to renew the experience and play again (see Fig. 5D). These two statistics are correlated and show that the children are engaged when they play the game.

6   Conclusion

In this paper we have proposed a new tool for capturing vivid and spontaneous children expressions by means of an engaging expression-related games. A mobile device is used in order to be able to realize recording session outside a lab environment. We think that capturing data in familiar setting reduces the bias brought by an unknown context. The game play encourages children to implicitly control the device orientation and light exposure in order to obtain high scores. The results of the preliminary study show that the children are enjoying the game experience and that they are ready and willing to renew the experience. As long as the facial expression are used as a mean of interaction within a rewarding context, engagement from subjects can be expected.

Preliminary results encourage us to extend the experiments to larger children corpus. As large quantity of data can be collected in out-of-lab conditions, it is important to assist the process of selecting viable data. Hence, we will focus on collecting and annotating processing. We envision to better quantify the quality of the recorded sessions by means of homogeneous illumination quantification, head orientation estimation, mobile device stability, etc. This metrics will enhance the annotation process by filtering inadequate conditions. At longer term we envision including new expression recognition techniques in order to propose more complex scenarios.

References

1. The MPLab GENKI database, GENKI-4K subset (2011)
2. Bartlett, M.S., Littlewort, G.C., Frank, M.G., Lainscsek, C., Fasel, I.R., Movellan, J.R.: Automatic recognition of facial actions in spontaneous expressions. J. Multimedia **1**(6), 22–35 (2006)
3. Batool, N., Chellappa, R.: Fast detection of facial wrinkles based on gabor features using image morphology and geometric constraints. PR **48**(3), 642–658 (2015)
4. Dalrymple, K.A., Gomez, J., Duchaine, B.: The dartmouth database of children's faces: acquisition and validation of a new face stimulus set. PLoS one **8**(11), e79131 (2013)
5. Danisman, T., Bilasco, I.M., Ihaddadene, N., Djeraba, C.: Automatic facial feature detection for facial expression recognition. In: VISAPP, vol. 2, pp. 407–412 (2010)
6. Danisman, T., Bilasco, I.M., Martinet, J., Djeraba, C.: Intelligent pixels of interest selection with application to facial expression recognition using multilayer perceptron. Sig. Process. **93**(6), 1547–1556 (2013)
7. Egger, H.L., Pine, D.S., Nelson, E., Leibenluft, E., Ernst, M., Towbin, K.E., Angold, A.: The NIMH child emotional faces picture set (NIMH-CHEFS): a new set of children's facial emotion stimuli. Int. J. Methods Psychiatr. Res. **20**(3), 145–156 (2011)
8. Ekman, P., Rosenberg, E.L.: What the Face Reveals: Basic and Applied Studies of Spontaneous Expression Using the Facial Action Coding System (FACS). Oxford University Press, Oxford (1997)
9. Lablack, A., Danisman, T., Bilasco, I.M., Djeraba, C.: A local approach for negative emotion detection. In: ICPR, pp. 417–420 (2014)
10. Lucey, P., Cohn, J.F., Kanade, T., Saragih, J., Ambadar, Z., Matthews, I.: The extended cohn-kanade dataset (CK+): a complete dataset for action unit and emotion-specified expression. In: CVPR-Workshops, pp. 94–101. IEEE (2010)
11. Lundqvist, D., Flykt, A., Öhman, A.: The Karolinska Directed Emotional Faces - KDEF, CD ROM from Department of Clinical Neuroscience, Psychology Section. Karolinska Institutet (1998). ISBN 91-630-7164-9
12. Lyons, M., Akamatsu, S., Kamachi, M., Gyoba, J.: Coding facial expressions with Gabor wavelets. In: FG, pp. 200–205. IEEE (1998)
13. McKeown, G., Valstar, M., Cowie, R., Pantic, M., Schroder, M.: The semaine database: annotated multimodal records of emotionally colored conversations between a person and a limited agent. IEEE Trans. Affect. Comput. **3**(1), 5–17 (2012)
14. Milborrow, S., Nicolls, F.: Locating facial features with an extended active shape model. In: Forsyth, D., Torr, P., Zisserman, A. (eds.) ECCV 2008. LNCS, vol. 5305, pp. 504–513. Springer, Heidelberg (2008). doi:10.1007/978-3-540-88693-8_37

15. Pérez-Espinosa, H., Reyes-García, C., Villaseñor-Pineda, L.: EmoWisconsin: an emotional children speech database in Mexican Spanish. In: D'Mello, S., Graesser, A., Schuller, B., Martin, J.-C. (eds.) ACII, Part II. LNCS, vol. 6975, pp. 62–71. Springer, Heidelberg (2011). doi:10.1007/978-3-642-24571-8_7
16. Phillips, P.J., Wechsler, H., Huang, J., Rauss, P.J.: The feret database and evaluation procedure for face-recognition algorithms. Image Vis. Comput. **16**(5), 295–306 (1998)
17. Ringeval, F., Sonderegger, A., Sauer, J., Lalanne, D.: Introducing the recola multimodal corpus of remote collaborative and affective interactions. In: FG, pp. 1–8. IEEE (2013)
18. Rowley, H.A., Baluja, S., Kanade, T.: Neural network-based face detection. IEEE Trans. Pattern Anal. Mach. Intell. **20**(1), 23–38 (1998)
19. Schuller, B., Batliner, A., Steidl, S., Seppi, D.: Recognising realistic emotions and affect in speech: state of the art and lessons learnt from the first challenge. Speech Commun. **53**(9), 1062–1087 (2011)
20. Shahid, S., Krahmer, E., Swerts, M.: Alone or together: exploring the effect of physical co-presence on the emotional expressions of game playing children across cultures. In: Markopoulos, P., Ruyter, B., IJsselsteijn, W., Rowland, D. (eds.) Fun and Games 2008. LNCS, vol. 5294, pp. 94–105. Springer, Heidelberg (2008). doi:10.1007/978-3-540-88322-7_10
21. Soleymani, M., Lichtenauer, J., Pun, T., Pantic, M.: A multimodal database for affect recognition and implicit tagging. IEEE Trans. Affect. Comput. **3**(1), 42–55 (2012)
22. Tian, Y.I., Kanade, T., Cohn, J.F.: Recognizing action units for facial expression analysis. PAMI **23**(2), 97–115 (2001)
23. Van Der Schalk, J., Hawk, S.T., Fischer, A.H., Doosje, B.: Moving faces, looking places: validation of the Amsterdam dynamic facial expression set (ADFES). Emotion **11**(4), 907 (2011)
24. Viola, P., Jones, M.: Rapid object detection using a boosted cascade of simple features. In: CVPR, vol. 1, pp. I-511–I-518 (2001)

Assessing Affective Dimensions of Play in Psychodynamic Child Psychotherapy via Text Analysis

Sibel Halfon[1], Eda Aydın Oktay[2], and Albert Ali Salah[2(✉)]

[1] Department of Psychology, Bilgi University, Istanbul, Turkey
sibel.halfon@bilgi.edu.tr
[2] Department of Computer Engineering, Boğaziçi University, Istanbul, Turkey
{eda.aydin,salah}@boun.edu.tr

Abstract. Assessment of emotional expressions of young children during clinical work is an important, yet arduous task. Especially in natural play scenarios, there are not many constraints on the behavior of the children, and the expression palette is rich. There are many approaches developed for the automatic analysis of affect, particularly from facial expressions, paralinguistic features of the voice, as well as from the myriads of non-verbal signals emitted during interactions. In this work, we describe a tool that analyzes verbal interactions of children during play therapy. Our approach uses natural language processing techniques and tailors a generic affect analysis framework to the psychotherapy domain, automatically annotating spoken sentences on valence and arousal dimensions. We work with Turkish texts, for which there are far less natural language processing resources than English, and our approach illustrates how to rapidly develop such a system for non-English languages. We evaluate our approach with longitudinal psychotherapy data, collected and annotated over a one year period, and show that our system produces good results in line with professional clinicians' assessments.

Keywords: Play therapy · Affect analysis · Psychotheraphy · Natural Language Processing · Turkish language · Valence · Arousal

1 Introduction

Clinical work with young children often relies on emotional expression and integration through symbolic play [58]. Play naturally provides a venue in which children can communicate and re-enact real or imagined experiences that are emotionally meaningful to them [23,52]. Many child therapists use play therapy to help children express their feelings, modulate affect, and resolve conflicts [16].

Affective analysis of psychodynamic play therapy sessions is a meticulous process, which requires many passes over the collected data to annotate different aspects of play behavior, and the markers of affective displays. Both the verbal

© Springer International Publishing AG 2016
M. Chetouani et al. (Eds.): HBU 2016, LNCS 9997, pp. 15–34, 2016.
DOI: 10.1007/978-3-319-46843-3_2

and non-verbal content of the interactions contain valuable information, and are analyzed in detail. Recent developments in multimedia analysis suggest that automatic tools could be used to help the analyst in these tasks. The advantages are many; such tools can support the therapist with immediate and rich feedback about the data, highlighting promising patterns for which more effort can be devoted, and also provide additional quantification of treatment effects. The disadvantages are that good automatic systems typically require a large amount of data for training, their generalization abilities may suffer from factors that may appear trivial to the experimenter (e.g. amount of ambient light, if a camera-based system is employed), and depending on the model used, justification of the classifications may be difficult to fathom.

In this work, we propose such an automatic, text-based tool for affective content analysis from verbal communications of children during play activity in psychodynamic treatment. Automatic analysis of psychodynamic play therapy is not a broadly researched subject, and we hope that our contribution will initiate more research in this domain. Another important point is that our tool is based on the Turkish language, which is spoken by more than 70 million people worldwide, but for which few analysis tools are available[1]. We make the developed tool available to the research community.

1.1 Preliminary Research Questions

It will be useful to put the work presented in this paper into the broader context of our research program. Using a naturalistic process-outcome design of psychodynamic play therapy with children at an outpatient clinic, our experimental study assessed affect expression over the course of treatment using two different kinds of instruments. Children's Play Therapy Instrument is a psychodynamically informed measure that aims to assess the structure and narrative of a child's play activity in psychotherapy [31]. The affective dimensions of the measure allows the rater to code an array of emotions expressed by the child while playing. The second instrument we use is the automated affective analysis model for Turkish language that analyzes affect from text using dimensions of Valence and Arousal [4]. Children's natural linguistic output over the course of treatment is assessed with the use of this instrument, and it is this second instrument that we describe in detail in this paper.

Given the paucity of research with clinical children in treatment, we report here a preliminary study which aims to investigate the utility of using an automatic text analysis tool to study the relations between affective expression in psychodynamic play therapy as it relates to different types of psychopathology and coping and its changes over the course of treatment. In terms of the type and quality of affective expression in play, literature shows that children with behavioral problems are likely to express more negative affect. However, there have been very few studies that looked at these associations with clinical samples

---

[1] Ethnologue estimates it as 71 millions as of 2006, related Wikipedia content suggests the numbers to be closer to 80 millions.

in therapy. The first aim of this study was to investigate the relations between the type and quality of affect expressed in play and its relation to type of psychopathology. Literature shows that different negative emotions relate differently to Internalizing and Externalizing Problem behaviors. In general, irritability and anger has been hypothesized to predict Externalizing Problem behaviors, whereas sadness, anxiety, and fear are believed to predict Internalizing Problems (see [20] for a review). Therefore, in our research, we specifically look at Internalizing and Externalizing children's expression of anger, sadness and anxiety in the initial stages of treatment, as well as over the course of treatment.

Secondly, studies show that the expression of negative affect in play is related to better coping in the long-run [53]. Play provides a context in which a child is able to explore both positive and negative emotional content in a safe, controlled manner. Play ultimately provides the opportunity to increase positive affect and reduce negative affect. However, empirical evidence to support this theory with clinical children over the course of treatment is limited. The second aim of this study was to assess the type of affect expressed in play over the course of psychodynamic play therapy and its relation to different kinds of psychopathological functioning.

Based on literature, several specific hypotheses can be tested for the initial phase of psychotherapy and over the course of treatment. The first hypothesis is that children with Externalizing Problems will show higher levels of anger and lower levels of valence. The second hypothesis is that children with Internalizing Problems will show higher levels of sadness, anxiety and lower levels of valence. Finally, we hypothesize that in the initial phase of therapy, both Internalizing and Externalizing children are expected to bring more negative affect (high anger, sadness and low valence) followed by more positive affect (high valence) over the course of treatment.

The two assessment instruments mentioned earlier, one used by psychologists, the second introduced in this paper, both aim to quantify affect over the course of the therapy for the investigation of these hypotheses.

The paper is structured as follows. In Sect. 2 we summarize related work in the area of affective expression in play. We broadly describe affect in psychotherapy research, specifically discuss the role of text analysis, and then briefly overview text analysis for sentiment and affect detection, which is a widely researched topic for multimedia and information retrieval. Section 3 introduces our text analysis system. Section 4 describes the data, and the participants of the study. Section 5 reports our experimental results, including sensitivity analysis for parameters of the system and ablation study for measuring the contribution of the different parts of the system. Finally, Sect. 6 concludes the paper.

2 Related Work

2.1 Affect in Psychotherapy Research with Children

Affect plays a significant role in psychotherapy, and a model of emotions can be used to explain different aspects of psychopathology [48]. In psychotherapy, the emphasis is on the analysis of affect rather than the elicitation of particular emotions, as the latter is quite difficult. Play therapy is one approach to obtain rich behavioral data with affective content.

There are numerous studies that link children's behavior in play to affective states. Children with disruptive behaviors have been shown to display more negative affect in their play and lower levels of affect regulation [11,17,59]. Dunn and Hughes found that children who were hyperactive and displayed conduct problems showed more physical aggression in their pretend games [19]. Similarly, children with disruptive behavior disorders such as Conduct Disorder and Attention Deficit Hyperactivity Disorder show more hostility and anger in their play [14]. Von Klitzing et al. found that expressing negative and/or aggressive affect in disorganized pretend play predicted behavior problems [63].

Russ and Cooperberg found that first and second graders who had more negative affect in their early play also had more symptoms of depression when measured 10 years later [51]. Additionally, in a sample of 322 six year-olds, some of whom were exposed to cocaine prior to birth, negative affect in play significantly correlated with both Internalizing and Externalizing behaviors [57]. Negative affect in play also correlated significantly with Major Depression Disorder and Oppositional Defiant Disorder in this study. These studies point to the importance of the relation between negative affect in play and behavioral problems. Some studies have also looked at the longitudinal effects of expression of affect, especially negative affect in play and behavioral functioning. Marcelo and Yates evaluated prospective relations among preschoolers' pretend play, coping flexibility, and behavior problems across varied degrees of child stress exposure [35]. They found that preschoolers who expressed more negative affect in their play engaged in more varied coping strategies (i.e., coping flexibility) during a simultaneous delay of gratification challenge and fewer Internalizing Problems one year later. These results show that even though expression of negative affect may initially be related to higher frequency of behavior problems, it may be related to enhanced coping in the long run [54].

However, there is a gap between the research literature that shows that affect in play facilitates coping, and the actual process of what happens in play therapy with clinical children in terms of affective changes. Bratton, Rhine and Jones, in a meta-analysis of outcome of play therapy, identified only seven studies that reported that play overall helped in the reduction of anxiety and fear [7]. The few empirical studies in the play intervention area that were focused on play with specific problems found that play reduced fears and anxiety for children with an acute physical illness and separation anxiety [5,41,47]. The research findings from a variety of studies in the child and adult areas suggest that other types of negative affect, like anger should also be helped by play therapies however these studies have not been carried out. There is even less research about the kinds of affective transformations that take place over the course of treatment. Gaensbauer and Siegel found that children who expressed affect in play, especially negative affect, were better able to work through their trauma in play-based therapy [26]. According to them, the key element that enables a child to use play adaptively, is the "degree to which the affects can be brought to the surface so the child can identify them and integrate them in more adaptive ways" (p. 297). Singer proposed that children can then increase positive affect and reduce negative affect through play [61]. This conceptualization fits with the idea that play is one way in which children learn to regulate their emotions. However, these ideas need to be empirically investigated.

2.2   Assessment Measures of Affect Expressed in Play Therapy

Even though there are many developmental measures to assess children's pretend play skills, there is relatively little evidence-based support for assessment measures that have been developed specifically to assess affective process and change in child play therapy. In particular, self-reported emotions are none too reliable, as they can be influenced by external factors [56].

Russ and Niec [54], in a review of play therapy assessment measures, talk about only three measures, which are Play Therapy Observation Instrument (PTOI) [28], the Trauma Play Scale [24] and the Children's Play Therapy Instrument (CPTI) [31], respectively. These are specifically designed to study children's expression of affect in therapy among other therapeutic indices. PTOI includes an Emotional Discomfort scale to rate child's comments about worries and troublesome events, inappropriate aggression toward the therapist, conflicted play, the quality and intensity of the child's affect (i.e., mood), and play disruption. The Trauma Play Scale allows for the coding of negative affect or lack of joy during play. CPTI has a more extensive affective component assessing affect regulation strategies as well as the types of affect expressed in play over the course of treatment. With all these measures, the sessions have to be recorded, transcribed and rated by trained judges on affective components.

2.3   Automatic Text Analyses of Affect from Text in Psychotherapy Research

A primary focus of the use of natural language processing (NLP) methods in psychotherapy has been to evaluate complex relational/emotional processes using the words from treatment sessions. Much of this work has involved the use of computerized dictionaries that place specific words in psychologically meaningful categories. For example, Anderson and colleagues found that when the patient used more emotion words, therapists obtained better outcomes when minimizing responses with cognitively geared verbs (e.g., "think," "believe," "know") [3]. Mergenthaler focused on the emotional tone (density of emotional words) and level of abstraction (the amount of abstract nouns) within patients' language and found that successful outcome in psychodynamic therapy is associated with increased use of emotion and abstraction in language, which shows that the patients have emotional access to conflictual themes and can reflect upon them [38,39].

Bucci's Referential Process theory is a similar, but more comprehensive psychological construct that "concerns the degree to which speakers (or writers) are able to access nonverbal, including emotional experience, in their own minds and to express this verbally in a form that is likely to evoke a corresponding experience in the listener" [9]). The affective connection between the language used and the underlying emotions has been consistently correlated with clinical ratings of psychoanalytic session effectiveness [10]. Pennebaker did not specifically investigate psychotherapy transcripts; however analyzed the writing features most strongly associated with enhanced psychological and physiological health found that people whose stories contained a high rate of what he called emotional processing words (e.g., "sad," "hurt," "guilt," "joy," "peace"), insight words (e.g., "realize," "understood," "thought," "know") and causal words (e.g., "because," "reason," "why") showed the greatest benefit from expressive writing exercises [45]. Even though there is substantial research in the application of NLP methods to specifically assess affective processes in adult treatment, to the best of our knowledge, no research has been carried out to adapt these measures to psychodynamic play therapy and there are no such resources in Turkish.

2.4 Text Analysis for Sentiment and Affect Detection

In multimedia computing, sentiment analysis and opinion mining refer to the categorization of a given text into positive, negative, or neutral classes, which makes it a relatively restricted and practicable NLP problem. On the other hand, detecting affect from text is a more challenging task, as it requires a profound understanding of both semantics and syntax of a language, as well as representing affect with the appropriate emotion categories or dimensions.

There exist several approaches to extract sentiment and opinion from textual multimedia content such as blogs, tweets, movie reviews and customer reviews. Basic methods include keyword spotting, lexical affinity, statistical NLP, learning based methods and commonsense-based approaches [13,44]. Similarly, methods for affective content analysis from text generally blend these approaches with rule-based systems. An example is the Affect Analysis Model, which analyzes affect specifically in informal online communication media [43]. This approach has five main steps; symbolic cue analysis, syntactic structure analysis, word-level, phrase-level and sentence-level analysis, respectively.

The majority of research on affect analysis from text relies on lexicon-based approaches, in which a set of keywords and associated affect categories are used to generate features for affect prediction models. One of the comprehensive lexical resources in this area is the Affective Norms for English Words (ANEW) corpus [6], which includes a set of normative emotional ratings for 1,034 commonly used English words. This tool represents a set of verbal materials that have been rated in terms of pleasure, arousal, and dominance to support emotion studies. Similarly, WordNet-Affect is a well known linguistic resource for extracting emotions from text [62]. The starting point of WordNet-Affect is to build a hierarchy of affective domain labels by labeling synsets (a set of one or more synonyms) that express affective concepts based on WordNet Domains [34].

A powerful system for text analysis is Linguistic Inquiry and Word Count (LIWC), which has a comprehensive affective dictionary to analyze text based on grammatical, psychological, and content word categorization. This dictionary allows to measure 74 different linguistic dimensions with more than 2,200 words and word stems. Affect sensing methods that are based on LIWC calculate word counts in the input text depending on these linguistic dimensions [27,30,46].

In addition to these lexicon-based approaches, several alternative methods have been studied in textual affect analysis. For example, Liu et al. first proposed the Commonsense-based approach by using three real-world commonsense databases [33]. Brooks et al. [8] presented an automated affect classification system in chat logs exploiting NLP and machine learning techniques. Their system segments the chat data and makes use of an improved bag-of-words model to classify text into 13 affect categories. The basic drawback of machine learning approaches is that they usually lack linguistic analysis by mainly focusing on statistical and syntactical features.

Recent approaches to text-based sentiment analysis rely on co-occurrence statistics, and in a multimedia context, typically combine image analysis with text [65]. To derive fixed length descriptors from variable length text fragments, the unsupervised Paragraph Vector approach proposed by Le and Mikolov is frequently used [32]. N-gram based generative approaches have shown some promise [40]. An example work for rule-based systems is Vader, which is tailored for social media text [29]. A recent review encompassing many application domains is given in [42].

3   The Proposed Text Analysis System

The automated affect analysis tool that is used in this work is designed to analyze affect and sentiment in Turkish online communication texts across domains [4]. Because of the lack of comprehensive Turkish corpora for affect analysis, we use an affect lexicon which is adapted from English to Turkish. English lemmas were gathered from the study of Warriner et al. [64], which evaluated 13,915 English lemmas in a nine point scale (1–9) by 1,827 participants through Mechanical Turk. For each item, mean and standard deviation values for valence, arousal, and dominance scores are given. Our text analysis model linearly transforms these affect scores to a five point scale [1–5]. Mapping to this range makes the scores given by the system directly comparable to the CPTI scores. The affective lexicon was expanded with synonym sets (synsets) from a standard Turkish dictionary (by TDK, Turkish Language Organization). As a result, a comprehensive affective lexicon for Turkish is developed, which includes valence, arousal, and dominance scores for 15,222 different words and phrases. We note here that the translation process naturally introduces errors, and ignores cultural aspects entirely. Nonetheless, this approach produces a useful resource with little cost.

To deal with written communication, the model uses additional resources, including 120 emoticons, 98 abbreviations, 50 interjections, and 71 modifiers (emotion intensifiers and diminishers). The affect analysis model of the tool is illustrated in Fig. 1.

In order to calculate sentence-level affect scores, the system first calculates the affective values of small units in the sentence, such as words and phrases, by

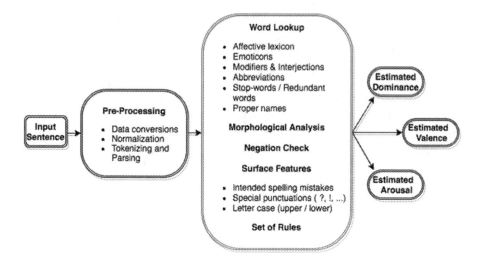

Fig. 1. Overview of the affect analysis system.

tokenizing the sentence into trigrams, bigrams and unigrams. Next, the system checks the modifier list. If there is any modifier connected to a verb or a noun as phrasal, the score of the word is updated based on the polarity of the sentence and on the particular coefficient of the modifier. Then, the system handles negation and some morphological alternations and updates the valence and arousal scores accordingly.

The system exploits some linguistic rules when calculating the overall sentence score, based on simplifying assumptions. For example, considering the transitive verbs in Turkish, for NN+VB structures, such as "hayatını kaybetti" (he lost his life), only the affective score of the verb is taken and then the noun is neutralized. Similarly, if there is a NN+ADJ structure such as "kafam karışık" (I'm confused), the noun is neutralized and only the adjective is taken into consideration. The overall sentence score is computed by summing the scores of these units. Only words with affective load are considered in the summation.

3.1 Adaptations for Psychotherapy

The initial design of this system targeted general online communications [4]. As a part of this work, we adapted the system to the psychotherapy domain by updating the affect dictionary. During the translation of the dictionary, the primary meanings were used for each word, but synonyms were also stored as alternatives. We checked approximately 1,500 words manually and selected the word with the most appropriate sense in the psychotherapy domain and discarded the others. Another feature that we added to the system is the detection of frequent stop-words and redundant words in play therapy. For example, words such as "anne" (mother), "baba" (father), "oyun" (play) have high valence scores in our dictionary, however, these words are mostly present with a neutral tone during the play sessions. Therefore, we neutralized the affect scores of these words when calculating the overall affect score. Stop-word and redundant word lists include more than 500 words that we have treated as neutral words. We suggest that to adapt the system for a different domain, expert knowledge should be integrated at this level. The resources and code developed for this work is made available.

We next describe the experimental setup. We evaluate our approach on data collected during psychotherapy sessions, and contrast our findings with those of the expert psychotherapists.

4   Experimental Setup

We describe the experimental setup somewhat extensively here; the reader may skip to Sect. 4.3 for the details of data analysis and results.

4.1   Data

Patients. The source of data used for this study comes from the Istanbul Bilgi University Psychotherapy Research Laboratory, which provides low-cost outpatient psychodynamic psychotherapy and professional training at master's level for students in the Clinical Psychology Program. Referrals were made by parents themselves or by mental health, medical, and child welfare professionals. The parents and the children were interviewed in order to determine whether the patients fit the study protocol inclusion criteria: ages between 4–10 years old; average intelligence; motivation for treatment; no psychotic symptoms; no significant developmental delays; no significant risk of suicide attempts; no drug abuse. The patients and their parents were extensively informed before commencing therapy and consented to video recordings and data collection at all times. The parents provided written informed consent and the children provided oral assent concerning use of their data for research purposes.

From September 2014 to September 2015, a group of 26 consecutively admitted patients who met inclusion criteria and consented to research were included in the study. 20 patients (76 %) completed the treatment. The demographics of the children are presented in Table 1. Eighty to ninety percent of the children come from low to middle socioeconomic status (SES) families and approximately 10 % of the parents are divorced or widowed for both samples. Referral Problems manifested primarily as anger management issues and behavioral problems, such as disobedience and not taking limits, followed by academic issues such as inattention in class and low grades and finally relational problems such as difficulties in family relationships or socialization with friends. At intake, 5 patients had DSM IV Attention Deficit and Hyperactivity Disorder, 3 patients had a Mood Disorder, 3 had Separation Anxiety Disorder, 2 patients had Encopresis.

Therapists. A total of 12 therapists (all clinical psychology master's level graduate students) treated the 20 patients, with each therapist generally working with one to two patients. The therapists were all females with ages ranging

Table 1. Subject characteristics at intake

Subject characteristics at intake		(N = 20)
Sex	Male	9
	Female	11
Age	4–6 years	8
	7–9 years	12
SES	Low	4
	Low - Middle	7
	Middle	5
	Middle - High	4
Referral Problem	Anxiety issues	2
	Behavioral/Anger problems	10
	Academic problem	7
	Relational problems	1

from 23 to 27 years. Each therapist was extensively educated in the theoretical background of psychodynamic play therapy and its various applications one year prior to the study. All therapists had the same experience level (1–2 years of psychotherapy training) and were supervised by experienced clinicians. In this way, the confounding variables rooted in differences in the educational background, experience, and supervision process were partially controlled.

Treatment. The treatment was psychodynamic play therapy. The treatment was not manualized and the only restrictions placed were regularity and length (once weekly treatment of 50 min for one year). Patients on average received 40 sessions. Even though there is no unitary model of therapeutic action in psychodynamic play therapy [25], the core principles and techniques employed can be summarized as follows: Central to this approach is the establishment of what is called a "setting". The psychotherapist sees the child at regular times, in the same play room with a standard set of play toys. This consistency provides a safe context that allows the child to play out difficult and disturbing emotional experiences that would be hard to express in the outside world. The exploration of the child's issues takes place in a largely child-led process way and the therapist encourages the child to express and reflect on his perceptions, feelings and thoughts in play. This is done by listening actively and inviting the child to continue his communications and asking questions about the play setting, temporal ordering, and the details of the characters, their thoughts, feelings and behaviors. The therapist also labels the repetitive themes, conflicts and feelings in play with the aim of helping the child to synthesize his experience. Interpretations aim to help the child see links between conflicting needs and emotions about self and others that find reflection in play behaviors and in the therapeutic relationship with the purpose of bringing to consciousness attitudes, assumptions and beliefs of which the child is unaware.

Session Selection. For correlational analyses, the longest play segments of the first two sessions of psychotherapy were used. A total of 40 sessions and 40 play segments constituted the data points for the analysis. To run Multi-level Modeling and Trend Analyses, a total of six sessions were selected from each case. To represent different therapy phases, the sessions were divided into early, middle, and late phase by dividing the total number of sessions for each case by three. Two consecutive sessions were selected from early therapy, two from late therapy, and two from the middle. Each session included 1 to 10 play segments (see Sect. 4.2), with a mean of 2.3. Up to four play segments were selected from each session in order to achieve a balance among participants, since the number of play segments per session varied. This sampling resulted in 120 sessions and 289 play segments for 20 children.

4.2   Measures

Background Information. Demographic information such as socioeconomic status and marital status were obtained using a standard intake information form and from information obtained in the initial interview.

Outcome Measures. The Child Behavior Checklist (CBCL) is a widely used method of identifying problematic behaviors in children [1]. For children ages 4 through 18, a parent or a primary caregiver reports on the child's academic performance, social relationships, and indicates how true a series of 112 problem behavior items are for the child on a 3 point scale (0 = not true, 1 = somewhat or sometimes true, and 2 = very true or often true). The following eight syndromes are scored from the CBCL, Anxious/Depressed, Withdrawn/ Depressed, Somatic Complaints, Social Problems, Thought Problems, Attention Problems, Rule Breaking Behavior, Aggressive Behavior. Anxious/Depressed, Withdrawn/Depressed, and Somatic Complaints syndromes comprise an Internalizing group, and the Rule Breaking Behavior and Aggressive Behavior syndromes comprise an Externalizing group, and Total Problems is the sum of scores on all problem items. The cut-off points for borderline and clinical designation are based on t–scores formed on a clinical population. Back translation, bilingual retest method, and pretest studies were used for the translation of the CBCL [22]. The test–retest reliability of the Turkish form was .84 for the Total Problems, and the internal consistency was adequate (Cronbach's alpha = .88; [21,22]).

Assessment of Affect in Play Activity. Children's Play Therapy Instrument (CPTI) is a psychodynamically-informed measure of in-session play activity [31]. The selected scales of the instrument for the purposes of the study involve Segmentation and Affects Expressed in Play (for further definition of play activity categories, see [15]). The CPTI rates children's behavior in a therapeutic setting at different levels. The first level involves a "Segmentation of the child's activity" (non-play, pre-play, play and interruption). Going forward, only play segments are rated. The Affective Component looks at the types emotions brought by the child to his play. Eight types of emotions are rated using a 5-point Likert scale: 5 = Most Characteristic; 4 = Considerable Evidence; 3 = Moderate Evidence; 2 = Minimal Evidence; 1 = No Evidence. For the purposes of the study, only Anger, Anxiety and Sadness were coded. Two masters level clinical psychology students, who received 20 hours of training on the CPTI by the first author and rated 10 training sessions (24 play segments) prior to the study, rated the sessions. They were independent assessors who were not associated with the treating clinicians or the cases, and blind to the purposes of the study. In order to identify the agreement level between judges for subscale ratings, Intra-class Correlation Coefficients (ICC) were computed. Cronbach Alpha was .72 for Segmentation, and .81 for Affect Types, suggesting good reliability for all Scales of CPTI.

Valence and Arousal. Categorical and dimensional modeling are two main approaches in representation of affect [12]. In dimensional modeling, the assumption is that emotions are related to each other and the affective state is investigated in a continuous multidimensional space, in generally two or three dimensions. There is still a lack of consensus on which dimensions are fundamental and which dimensions are a mixture of these basic dimensions. However, the popular Circumplex model of emotions [49], which defines "valence" and "arousal" as the principal axes, is frequently used. Valence describes the extent of pleasure (positive) and sadness (negative), and arousal (or activation) describes the extent of calmness and excitation [49,55]. Valence and arousal are commonly considered as independent dimensions, however, real-world findings confirm that these two dimensions are correlated most of the time.

4.3   Method of Automatic Analysis

As a general rule, linguistic programs need to segment the transcript (typically in equally sized units) for comparison of the data while analyzing a text. As the proposed text analysis tool performs sentence level analysis, firstly we had to segment sessions into smaller units. The length of a scoring unit containing the minimum number of necessary words is determined by statistical procedures described before [36]. In psychotherapy research, an entry with minimum of 150 words is required by many linguistic programs such as the therapeutic Cycle Model and computer-assisted content analysis [37]. Therefore, for the grouping, we created 150-word chunks of sentences while paying attention to play segment borders. Each 150 word block was processed as a single sentence in our affect analysis system. Then, average scores of these 150 word blocks gave us the overall affect score of the corresponding therapy session.

5   Results

5.1   Descriptive Statistics

To examine the association between CBCL problems and affect expressed in play at the beginning of therapy, play affect scores as measured by CPTI Anger, Anxiety and Sadness scores, VA (Valence and Arousal) scores collected in the initial two sessions of psychotherapy were calculated. Each child's two longest play segment affect scores from the initial two sessions were computed, which gave mean affect scores for the initial phase of psychotherapy. The means and standard deviations for each of the major variables collected at the beginning of psychotherapy are listed in Table 2. The first two rows (Valence and Arousal) are obtained by the proposed automatic analysis approach, and the next three rows are CPTI annotations (Anger, Anxiety and Sadness).

Prior to testing correlations, the possible contribution of background and demographic variables to the studied variables was examined through preliminary analyses. Spearman correlations were conducted to assess the association of age and gender with the main study variables: CBCL Problems and all CPTI Items and VA. No significant differences were found according to these variables.

Table 2. Descriptive statistics for affect variables and CBCL problems (N = 20)

	Affect variables	
Variable	M	SD
Valence	3.48	0.38
Arousal	3.54	0.71
Anger	2.71	0.87
Anxiety	3.03	0.61
Sadness	1.4	0.42
	CBCL problems (T Scores)	
Externalizing Problems	61.80	8.70
Internalizing Problems	59.95	11.14

5.2   Preliminary Results of Affect Analysis at the Beginning of Treatment

The relationship between the CBCL Problems and play affect scores as measured by CPTI Anger, Anxiety and Sadness scores and Valence and Arousal scores collected in the initial two sessions of psychotherapy were examined. Due to the low number of children included in the analysis, Spearman Correlations were used (see Table 2).

Results show that in the first two sessions, CPTI Anger scores were positively related to Externalizing Problems, Valence scores were negatively related to

Table 3. Spearman correlations between the affect scores and CBCL problems.

	CPTI anxiety	CPTI sadness	CPTI anger	VA valence	VA arousal
CBCL					
Internalizing Prob	−.343	.218	−.014	−.495[a]	−.644[b]
Externalizing Prob	−.011	−.025	.496[a]	−.517[a]	.253

Note: [a] Correlation is significant at the .05 level; [b] Correlation is significant at the .01 level.

Internalizing and Externalizing Problems, and Arousal Scores were negatively related to Internalizing Problems on the CBCL. No significance was observed for CPTI Sadness and Anxiety scores (see Table 3).

While we do not analyze the specific findings of the play therapy sessions in detail here, we note that the high correlations obtained by the proposed automatic tool and the manual CPTI coding are very promising. The results provide empirical support for two measures of affective assessment that can be used towards investigating affective processes in play in psychodynamic play therapy. Both CPTI and Valence-Arousal showed preliminary promise for systematic play observation.

5.3 Preliminary Analyses of Affect Expressed During Treatment

In order to assess affect expressed during the treatment, two sessions from the beginning, middle and end of therapy were used. As such the data consisted of 6 sessions from 20 children resulting in 120 sessions and 289 play segments. We conducted Hierarchical Linear Modelling (HLM) [50] which is used to measure data that has more than one level. Using Hierarchical Linear Growth Curve Modeling, affective change over time was modeled. This model takes into account the hierarchical structure of the data i.e., different measurements in time (level 1) are nested within subjects (level 2). Using maximum likelihood, multilevel analysis allows for missing data [60]. Effect-sizes were calculated using R2.

To see the variability of mean valence, arousal and anger scores, first null models were run for each. Results showed that Valence ($\beta= 3.39$, t(19) $= 124.36$, p < 0.001), Arousal ($\beta = 3.54$, t(19) $= 41.64$, p < 0.001) and Anger ($\beta = 2.59$, t(19) $= 18.09$, p < 0.001) significantly varied across participants.

Results also revealed that left over variance was significant for Arousal (Var(u_0) $= 0.08$, χ^2 (19) $= 49.49$, p < 0.001), Anger (Var(u_0) $= 0.27$, χ^2 (19)$= 54.36$, p < 0.001), but not for Valence (Var(u_0)$= 0.00$, $\chi^2(19)=15.34$, p >0.05). We also calculated how much of the variance is explained by level 2 variables (Externalizing and Internalizing problems) in predicting Valence, Arousal and CPTI Anger. To calculate this we used the following formula:

$$Explained\ variance = \frac{u_0\ (unconditional) - u_0\ (conditional)}{u_0\ (unconditional)} \qquad (1)$$

Because HLM does not give a direct R2 value, the variance explained with this formula can be used as pseudo R2 [2].

We found that for Arousal 16 % and for Anger 19 % of the variance is explained by Externalizing and Internalizing Problems. For Valence, we. could not obtain a value because left over variance was not significant at null model as stated above. Together, these results indicated that further analysis using Hierarchical Linear Modeling, was suited. •

Growth Curve Analyses. To investigate the change in Internalizing and Externalizing children's Valence, Arousal and Anger scores across sessions, time and time squared variables were entered into the model at level 1 to see the linear and quadratic growth rates of variables. For Internalizing Problems, results revealed a significant linear increase ($\beta = 0.05$, t(161) = 2.98, p < 0.05) in Valence as well as Arousal ($\beta = 0.06$, t(161) = 2.17, p < 0.05) scores. Effect sizes for each trend was small (R2 = 0.01). No significance was observed for linear ($\beta = -0.02$, t(161) = 0.18, p >0.05) and quadratic effect for CPTI Anger ($\beta = -0.03$, t(161) = 0.58, p >0.05). Growth rates of Valence, Arousal and CPTI Anger with Externalizing Problems were not significant.

5.4 Ablation Study

We assess the impact of different parameters on the accuracy of our affect prediction system. To achieve that, we setup a sentence-level annotation with 4 different play therapy sessions that includes approximately 500 sentences in total. For each sentence, a human annotator assigned a Valence and an Arousal score by using a 5-point Likert scale. After the automated affect analysis, we compared the model prediction scores with the ground truth scores that we obtained from the annotation. Model scores are also scaled continuously between 1 and 5. In order to calculate the accuracy, we mapped the Valence scores to positive (>3) and negative (< 3) classes to carry out the corresponding classification of the affect.

The first experiment we conducted tested the benefit of using domain adaptation on the text analysis system. As can be seen from Table 4, with the updated dictionary and redundant word elimination, we observed a higher correlation and reduced mean square error in both Valence and Arousal dimensions.

Table 4. The effect of adapted dictionary for psychotherapy domain

	Valence		Arousal	
Measure	Adapted Dict.	Generic Dict.	Adapted Dict.	Generic Dict.
Correlation (P < 0.01)	0.58	0.32	0.33	0.23
Mean square error	0.24	0.39	0.51	0.58

Table 5. The accuracy of the model for binary Valence classification

	Accuracy (%)
All features	**83.5**
All features with generic dictionary	74.5
All features without redundant words	81.1
All features without negation	75.1
All features without modifiers	79.8

Contribution of the different parts of the system to the performance is given in Table 5. Our results show that the system gives the best accuracy (83 %) when all features are employed with the adapted dictionary for psychotherapy domain. We see that eliminating the domain-specific redundant words improves the system performance by 2 %.

6   Conclusions

There is relatively little empirical investigation of the measurement of affect expressed in play and how it relates to psychopathology during the treatment process of children in psychodynamic play therapy. We propose in this paper an automatic rule-based text analysis tool that can quantify Valence and Arousal for longitudinal transcriptions of therapy sessions. We obtain good agreement with a standard measure used by psychotherapists. Result of the study support the relationships between affect expressed in play and behavioral problems as well as the importance of play in the modulation of negative feelings. The findings were consistent with our prediction which indicated Internalizing and Externalizing Problems negatively associated with Valence at the beginning of treatment. These findings parallel previous results from the literature that suggest a relationship between negative affect in play and maladaptive behavior. Our findings also indicated, in line with previous literature, that children with Internalizing Problems present with a constricted range of negative affect and can use psychodynamic play therapy towards the modulation of negative affect in play. They are able to express more intense and positive emotions over the course of treatment as shown in the increase in Arousal scores. These findings provide preliminary empirical support for two measures of affective assessment that can be used towards investigating affective processes in play in psychodynamic play therapy.

One of the main limitations of the study is that none of the existing text-based sentiment analysis approaches could be directly employed for comparative assessment, as few approaches are proposed for Turkish (see [4] and references therein). It is obvious that improvements in the automatic affect analysis pipeline will translate to more reliable assessment of the play therapy sessions. In particular, a comprehensive affective lexicon prepared for Turkish language would be useful. The work by Dehkharghani et al. towards preparing such a resource is a good step forward [18], but currently it is in a preliminary stage, and the translated (but more extensive) dictionary we have used produces more accurate results [4].

Our work also indicates that it is possible to adapt sentiment analysis resources developed for one language (i.e. English, in this case) for a system designed for processing another language. N-gram and co-occurrence based approaches do not have this flexibility, and need to be trained directly with resources of the language they are meant to process. Subsequently, the proposed approach presents a possibility of supporting and complementing these methods.

Acknowledgments. This study is partially supported by the Scientific and Technological Research Council of Turkey (TUBITAK) grants 114E481 and 215K180.

References

1. Achenbach, T.M.: Manual for the Child Behavior Checklist/4-18 and 1991 profile. Department of Psychiatry, University of Vermont Burlington, VT (1991)
2. Anderson, D.: Hierarchical linear modeling (HLM): an introduction to key concepts within cross-sectional and growth modelling frameworks. Behavioral Research and Teaching, Oregon (2012)
3. Anderson, T., Bein, E., Pinnell, B., Strupp, H.: Linguistic analysis of affective speech in psychotherapy: a case grammar approach. Psychother. Res. **9**(1), 88–99 (1999)
4. Aydın Oktay, E., Balcı, K., Salah, A.A.: Automatic assessment of dimensional affective content in Turkish multi-party chat messages. In: Proceedings of the International Workshop on Emotion Representations and Modelling for Companion Technologies, pp. 19–24. ACM (2015)
5. Barnett, L.A., Storm, B.: Play, pleasure, and pain: the reduction of anxiety through play. Leis. Sci. **4**(2), 161–175 (1981)
6. Bradley, M.M., Lang, P.J.: Affective norms for English words (ANEW): instruction manual and affective ratings. Technical report, C-1, The Center for Research in Psychophysiology, Univ. of Florida (1999)
7. Bratton, S.C., Ray, D., Rhine, T., Jones, L.: The efficacy of play therapy with children: a meta-analytic review of treatment outcomes. Prof. Psychol. Res. Pract. **36**(4), 376 (2005)
8. Brooks, M., Kuksenok, K., Torkildson, M.K., Perry, D., Robinson, J.J.,Scott, T.J., Anicello, O., Zukowski, A., Harris, P., Aragon, C.R.: Statistical affect detection in collaborative chat. In: Proceedings of CSCW, pp. 317–328. ACM (2013)
9. Bucci, W., Maskit, B.: Beneath the surface of the therapeutic interaction: the psychoanalytic method in modern dress. J. Am. Psychoanal. Assoc. **55**(4), 1355–1397 (2007)
10. Bucci, W., Maskit, B., Murphy, S.: Connecting emotions, words: the referential process. Phenomenol. Cogn. Sci. **15**, 1–25 (2015)
11. Butcher, J.L., Niec, L.N.: Disruptive behaviors and creativity in childhood: the importance of affect regulation. Creativity Res. J. **17**(2–3), 181–193 (2005)
12. Calvo, R.A., Mac Kim, S.: Emotions in text: dimensional and categorical models. Comput. Intell. **29**(3), 527–543 (2013)

13. Cambria, E., Schuller, B., Xia, Y., Havasi, C.: New avenues in opinion mining and sentiment analysis. IEEE Intell. Syst. **28**(2), 15–21 (2013)
14. Casey, R.J.: Emotional competence in children with externalizing and internalizing disorders. Emotional Development in a Typical Children, pp. 161–183 (1996)
15. Chazan, S.: Profiles of Play: Assessing and Observing Structure and Process in Play Therapy. Jessica Kingsley Publishers, London (2002)
16. Chethik, M.: Techniques of Child Therapy: Psychodynamic Strategies. Guilford Press, New York (2003)
17. D'Angelo, L.: Child's play: the relationship between the use of play and adjustment styles. Unpublished Doctoral Dissertation (1995)
18. Dehkharghani, R., Saygin, Y., Yanikoglu, B., Oflazer, K.: SentiTurkNet: a Turkish polarity lexicon for sentiment analysis. Lang. Resour. Eval. **50**, 1–19 (2015)
19. Dunn, J., Hughes, C.: I got some swords and you're dead! Violent fantasy, antisocial behavior, friendship, and moral sensibility in young children. Child Dev. **72**(2), 491–505 (2001)
20. Eisenberg, N., Cumberland, A., Spinrad, T.L., Fabes, R.A., Shepard, S.A., Reiser, M., Murphy, B.C., Losoya, S.H., Guthrie, I.K.: The relations of regulation and emotionality to children's externalizing and internalizing problem behavior. Child Dev. **72**(4), 1112–1134 (2001)
21. Erol, N., Arslan, B., Akçakın, M.: The adaptation, standardization of the child behavior checklist among 6–18 year-old Turkish children. Eunethdis: European Approaches to Hyperkinetic Disorder, pp. 97–113 (1995)
22. Erol, N., Şimşek, Z.T.: Mental health of Turkish children: behavioral and emotional problems reported by parents, teachers, and adolescents. Int. Perspect. Child Adolesc. Ment. Health **1**, 223–247 (2000)
23. Fein, G.G.: Pretend play: creativity and consciousness. In: Gorlitz, P., Wohlwill, J. (eds.) Curiosity, Imagination, and Play, pp. 281–304. Lawrence Erlbaum Associates, Hillsdale (1987)
24. Findling, J.H., Bratton, S.C., Henson, R.K.: Development of the trauma play scale: an observation-based assessment of the impact of trauma on play therapy behaviors of young children. Int. J. Play Ther. **15**(1), 7 (2006)
25. Fonagy, P., Target, M.: The place of psychodynamic theory in developmental psychopathology. Dev. Psychopathol. **12**(03), 407–425 (2000)
26. Gaensbauer, T.J., Siegel, C.H.: Therapeutic approaches to posttraumatic stress disorder in infants and toddlers. Infant Ment. Health J. **16**(4), 292–305 (1995)
27. Hancock, J.T., Landrigan, C., Silver, C.: Expressing emotion in text-based communication. In: Proceedings of the SIGCHI Conference on Human Factors in Computing Systems, pp. 929–932. ACM (2007)
28. Howe, P.A., Silvern, L.E.: Behavioral observation of children during play therapy: preliminary development of a research instrument. J. Pers. Assess. **45**(2), 168–182 (1981)
29. Hutto, C.J., Gilbert, E.: Vader: a parsimonious rule-based model for sentiment analysis of social media text. In: Eighth International AAAI Conference on Weblogs and Social Media (2014)
30. Kahn, J.H., Tobin, R.M., Massey, A.E., Anderson, J.A.: Measuring emotional expression with the linguistic inquiry and word count. Am. J. Psychol. **120**, 263–286 (2007)
31. Kernberg, P., Chazan, S., Normandin, L.: The children's play therapy instrument (CPTI): description, development, and reliability studies. J. Psychother. Pract. Res. **7**(3), 196–207 (1997)

32. Le, Q.V., Mikolov, T.: Distributed representations of sentences and documents. ICML **14**, 1188–1196 (2014)
33. Liu, H., Lieberman, H., Selker, T.: A model of textual affect sensing using real-world knowledge. In: Proceedings of IUI, pp. 125–132. ACM (2003)
34. Magnini, B., Cavaglia, G.: Integrating subject field codes into WordNet. In: LREC (2000)
35. Marcelo, A.K., Yates, T.M.: Prospective relations among preschoolers' play, coping, and adjustment as moderated by stressful events. J. Appl. Dev. Psychol. **35**(3), 223–233 (2014)
36. Mergenthaler, E.: Textbank Systems: Computer Science Applied in the Field of Psychoanalysis. Springer Science and Business Media, Berlin (1985)
37. Mergenthaler, E.: Computer-assisted content analysis. Nachtrichten Spezial, pp. 3–32 (1996)
38. Mergenthaler, E.: Emotion-abstraction patterns in verbatim protocols: a new way of describing psychotherapeutic processes. J. Consult. Clin. Psychol. **64**(6), 1306–1315 (1996)
39. Mergenthaler, E.: Cycles of emotion-abstraction patterns: a way of practice oriented process research? Br. Psychol. Soc. Psychother. Sect. Newsl. **24**, 16–29 (1998)
40. Mesnil, G., Mikolov, T., Ranzato, M., Bengio, Y.: Ensemble of generative and discriminative techniques for sentiment analysis of movie reviews. In: ICLR (2014)
41. Milos, M.E., Reiss, S.: Effects of three play conditions on separation anxiety in young children. J. Consult. Clin. Psychol. **50**(3), 389 (1982)
42. Mohammad, S.M.: Sentiment analysis: detecting valence, emotions, and other affectual states from text. Emotion Measurement (2016)
43. Neviarouskaya, A., Prendinger, H., Ishizuka, M.: Affect analysis model: novel rule-based approach to affect sensing from text. Nat. Lang. Eng. **17**(01), 95–135 (2011)
44. Pang, B., Lee, L.: Opinion mining and sentiment analysis. Found. Trends Inf. Retrieval **2**(1–2), 1–135 (2008)
45. Pennebaker, J.W., Chung, C.K.: Expressive writing, emotional upheavals, and health. Foundtions of Health Psychology, pp. 263–284 (2007)
46. Pennebaker, J.W., Mehl, M.R., Niederhoffer, K.G.: Psychological aspects of natural language use: our words, our selves. Ann. Rev. Psychol. **54**(1), 547–577 (2003)
47. Phillips, R.D.: Whistling in the dark? A review of play therapy research. Psychother. Theor. Res. Pract. Train. **22**(4), 752 (1985)
48. Plutchik, R.: Emotions in the practice of psychotherapy: clinical implications of affect theories. American Psychological Association, Washington, D.C (2000)
49. Posner, J., Russell, J.A., Peterson, B.S.: The circumplex model of affect: an integrative approach to affective neuroscience, cognitive development, and psychopathology. Dev. Psychopathol. **17**(3), 715–734 (2005)
50. Raudenbush, S., Bryk, A., Seltzer, M., Congden, R.: An Introduction to HLM: Computer Program and User's Guide. Department of Education, University of Chicago, Chicago (1986)
51. Russ S., Cooperberg, M.: Play as a predictor of creativity, coping and depression in adolescence. Manuscript Submitted for Publication (2002)
52. Russ, S.W.: Affect and Creativity: The Role of Affect and Play in the Creative Process. Psychology Press, Hove (1993)
53. Russ, S.W.: Play in Child Development, Psychotherapy: Toward Empirically Supported Practice. Routledge, London (2003)
54. Russ, S.W., Niec, L.N.: Play in Clinical Practice: Evidence-Based Approaches. Guilford Press, New York (2011)

55. Russell, J.A.: Culture and the categorization of emotions. Psychol. Bull. **110**(3), 426 (1991)
56. Schachter, S., Singer, J.: Cognitive, social, and physiological determinants of emotional state. Psychol. Rev. **69**(5), 379–399 (1962)
57. Scott, T.J.L., Short, E.J., Singer, L.T., Russ, S.W., Minnes, S.: Psychometric properties of the dominic interactive assessment a computerized self-report for children. Assessment **13**(1), 16–26 (2006)
58. Shirk, S.R., Russell, R.L.: Change Processes in Child Psychotherapy: Revitalizing Treatment and Research. Guilford Press, New York (1996)
59. Singer, D.G., Singer, J.L.: The House of make-believe: Children's Play and the Developing Imagination. Harvard University Press, Cambridge (1990)
60. Singer, J.D., Willett, J.B.: Applied Longitudinal Data Analysis: Modeling Change and Event Occurrence. Oxford University Press, Oxford (2003)
61. Singer, J.L.: Imaginative play in childhood: precursor of subjunctive thoughts, daydreaming, and adult pretending games. The Future of Play Theory, pp. 187–219 (1995)
62. Strapparava, C., Valitutti, A.: WordNet affect: an affective extension of WordNet. LREC **4**, 1083–1086 (2004)
63. Von Klitzing, K., Kelsay, K., Emde, R.N., Robinson, J., Schmitz, S.: Gender-specific characteristics of 5-year-olds' play narratives and associations with behavior ratings. J. Am. Acad. Child Adolesc. Psychiatry **39**(8), 1017–1023 (2000)
64. Warriner, A.B., Kuperman, V., Brysbaert, M.: Norms of valence, arousal, and dominance for 13,915 English lemmas. Behav. Res. Methods **45**(4), 1191–1207 (2013)
65. You, Q., Luo, J., Jin, H., Yang, J.: Joint visual-textual sentiment analysis with deep neural networks. In: Proceedings of the 23rd ACM International Conference on Multimedia, MM 2015, New York, pp. 1071–1074. ACM (2015)

Multimodal Detection of Engagement in Groups of Children Using Rank Learning

Jaebok Kim[1(✉)], Khiet P. Truong[1], Vicky Charisi[1], Cristina Zaga[1], Vanessa Evers[1], and Mohamed Chetouani[2]

[1] Human Media Interaction, University of Twente, Enschede, The Netherlands
{j.kim,k.p.truong,v.charisi,c.zaga,v.evers}@utwente.nl
[2] Sorbonne Universités, UPMC Univ Paris 06, CNRS UMR 7222,
Institut des Systémes Intelligents et de Robotique (ISIR),
4 Place Jussieu, 75005 Paris, France
mohamed.chetouani@upmc.fr

Abstract. In collaborative play, children exhibit different levels of engagement. Some children are engaged with other children while some play alone. In this study, we investigated multimodal detection of individual levels of engagement using a ranking method and non-verbal features: turn-taking and body movement. Firstly, we automatically extracted turn-taking and body movement features in naturalistic and challenging settings. Secondly, we used an ordinal annotation scheme and employed a ranking method considering the great heterogeneity and temporal dynamics of engagement that exist in interactions. We showed that levels of engagement can be characterised by relative levels between children. In particular, a ranking method, Ranking SVM, outperformed a conventional method, SVM classification. While either turn-taking or body movement features alone did not achieve promising results, combining the two features yielded significant error reduction, showing their complementary power.

Keywords: Children · Engagement · Social Signal Processing · Non-verbal behaviours

1 Introduction

Engagement is often defined as the process of maintaining connections between participants through exchanges of verbal and non-verbal attentional cues to each other [5,35]. From preschool age onwards, children play with peers in small groups [31,32] where inter-group dynamics lead to varying engagement behaviours with children [2,22,37]. For example, one child does not play with others but plays alone while another child interacts substantially and gets involved with the other children in the group.

Recent advances in the automatic detection of engagement are more and more facilitating the development of robots able to support social interactions among

© Springer International Publishing AG 2016
M. Chetouani et al. (Eds.): HBU 2016, LNCS 9997, pp. 35–48, 2016.
DOI: 10.1007/978-3-319-46843-3_3

children [34]. Our aim is to endow a social robot with the ability to anticipate children's level of engagement and to interact with children during playful tasks, and this paper introduces a novel approach to the automatic detection of individual engagement during child-child interaction. Our approach focuses on the analysis of children's non-verbal behaviours which are strong cues of engagement [5,38].

The automatic analysis and detection of engagement have been studied before using multi-modal cues such as speech activity, gaze, posture, and gestures [4,6, 19,21,29]. These features can be categorised into vocal and visual features, and each category has its own strengths and drawbacks in the wild. For example, vocal features are not useful in situations where there is no speech, which often occur during children's playful tasks. Moreover, visual features such as gaze and gesture have limited accuracy depending on view points and distances. These challenges should be addressed to achieve reliable performances in naturalistic settings where we cannot instruct or restrict the behaviours of the children.

Furthermore, overlooked aspects in previous studies are temporal and group dynamics. Even in group play, an engagement level of each child is modelled by only his own non-verbal behaviours although their engagement and non-verbal behaviours are strongly interrelated with those of the other participants [2,22]. In other words, a child's level of engagement is shaped by the other participants engagement and it may greatly vary depending on the group composition. Moreover, engagement levels vary over period (i.e. temporal dynamics), which calls for an analysis with fine time resolutions.

In this paper, we present multimodal detection of individual engagement of children in a naturalistic environment. To address the inevitable challenges such as silent moments and noisy viewpoints, we utilised not only vocalic turn-taking features but also body movement features. Moreover, we designed an ordinal annotation scheme and adopted a ranking method considering the great heterogeneity and temporal dynamics of engagement that exist in interactions [2,22].

This paper is structured as follows. In Sect. 2, details of the related works will be presented. We will describe our audiovisual corpus and annotation scheme in Sect. 3. We will explain our method and features in Sect. 4. In Sect. 5, the results of our experiments will be presented, and conclusions will be addressed in Sect. 6.

2   Related Work

The automatic detection of engagement using multi-modal cues has been investigated in the field of Human Robot Interaction (HRI) and Social Signal Processing (SSP) [4,35,38]. In [29], hand-coded features such as speech, gaze, gesture, and postures of two children were utilised to model individual and group-level engagement. Their F-score based feature ranking showed that gaze-related features were more discriminative than other features (e.g. posture and smiling). Although their feature extraction was based on a fine-temporal resolution (500 ms), the authors did not model turn-taking between children. In [6], a correlation between body movement and engagement in playful gaming situations was investigated. The amount of body movements was quantified by the normalized sum of the angular movements over the total duration of play. They found a positive correlation between the movement and engagement while relying on wearable motion capturing devices which are expensive for practical applications. Moreover, group-level involvement, i.e. the average of individual engagement, was modelled using pitch, hand-coded gaze and blinking [7]. In [19], acoustic features (e.g. energy, pitch, speaking rate) and body movement features (e.g. amount of movements, orientation of head and hands) were automatically extracted to detect group-level engagement.

Although turn-taking features were often neglected in the aforementioned studies, turn-taking features, showed a positive relation to engagement [5,13]. While individual speaking activity is not often informative to detect engagement, comprehensive behaviours such as speaker-changes, overlaps, and interruptions, demonstrated promising performances in the detection of engagement [28]. However, the performances of turn-taking features still remain doubtful in naturalistic settings where silent situations often occur.

While the HRI studies [4,29] revealed that gaze-oriented movements and hand gestures were related to engagement, the settings often had regulations on behaviours of subjects or relied on hand-coded features. Without any regulation, the automatic extraction of these features is limited in naturalistic settings. Unlike in these features, body movements are atomic primitives which do not contain any contextual or sequence knowledge of human behaviours such as engagement [1,8]; however, their statistics (e.g. occurrences) are known to be related with engagement [6,17]. Moreover, the extraction of body movements is the first step to look into more advanced features (e.g. gaze and gesture). Hence, robust methods to extract and segment movements have been developed (e.g. Motion History Image (MHI) and K-means based segmentation) for identifying individuals in a group [1,3,8].

To resolve large variations of human behaviours, a large amount of data is often required, which is challenging for our targeted scenarios where a group of children exhibit social interactions in natural settings. Instead of collecting a large corpus, pairwise based ranking methods, for example, Ranking SVM, can be used to resolve these variations since these methods learn differences between instances in given conditions [23,26]. For example, Ranking SVM achieved significant improvement compared to conventional methods (e.g. classification) in speech emotion recognition and engagement detection [14,28]. However, none of these studies revealed limitations in silent situations which are common in child-child interactions.

These studies did not deal with the naturalistic settings where spontaneous interactions without restrictions and inter-group dynamics occur, and these challenges must be addressed to develop practical applications of engagement detection. To resolve the challenges, the annotation scheme, learning methods, and features adopted in this study will be elaborated on in the following sections.

3   Data

We used a corpus containing audiovisual recordings of groups of children [27]. In our corpus, a playful task was used to facilitate children's natural social

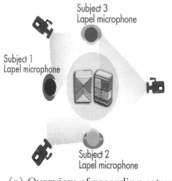

(a) Overview of recording setup   (b) Video still of corpus

Fig. 1. Naturalistic audiovisual corpus used in our study

behaviours. Using 3D cubes, children were asked to build given shapes of animals in collaborative ways as shown in Fig. 1. Dutch children aged 5–8 (6.95 ± .95) were recruited from a primary school. We clustered the children by age and then randomly assigned them to a group of three for each session. Eight out of ten sessions were considered in our analyses (two sessions were discarded due to malfunctions of recording), totalling approximately 3 h. Although we recorded children's behaviours using three different viewpoints focusing on each child as shown in Fig. 1(a), occlusions caused by children sitting close to each other occurred relatively often which posed a great challenge to the automatic extraction of individual body movement features. Since we did not restrict the movement of the children (except for initial positions), they often moved around and interacted with each other, which led to noisy data.

3.1 Annotation

For our task, we define engagement as verbal and non-verbal exchanges of attention, i.e. attending and responding to each other in a group [28]. During our pilot coding sessions, we provided two coders with the definition of engagement and videos of three sessions. We asked them to label individual levels of engagement in an absolute manner ({low, medium, high}). It turned out that annotators had difficulty labelling these classes, resulting in poor inter-rater agreement (kappa) between the two coders (.57). Hence, we established an annotation scheme by considering relative levels of engagement as follows (from low to high level) [28]:

1 giving relatively less attention to others and receiving relatively less attention from others.
2a giving relatively less attention to others but receiving attention from others.
2b giving attention to others but receiving relatively less attention from others.
3 giving attention to others and receiving attention from others.

In this way, children can be ordered from a low to a high level of engagement. For subsequent analyses, the classes: {2a} and {2b} were equally ranked (in level

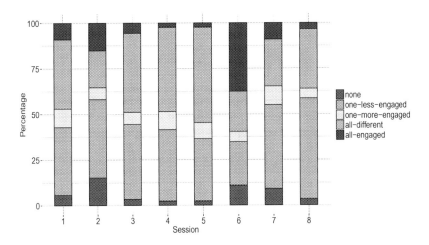

Fig. 2. Distribution of engagement situations

of engagement) and merged into one class {2}. Moreover, if any differences could not be observed among the three children, ties were allowed (e.g. {1, 1, 1}, {3, 3, 3}). In order to annotate all the recordings, a proper size for an annotation segment needed to be determined. Through pilot coding sessions, we concluded on an empirical basis that 5s-long segments were suitable for the annotators to observe various levels of engagement. The videos and description of relative levels of engagement were given to two annotators to code each child for level every 5 s using ELAN [39]. Finally, the average of inter-rater agreement was 0.82 (kappa). In subsequent analyses, we used 1510 segments that both annotators agreed upon which included silent segments ($<22.5\%$).

If children are equally engaged or disengaged with each other in general, our ordinal annotation is not meaningful. To investigate this issue, we analysed five types of engagement situations: "no-one-engaged (none)", "one-less-engaged", "one-more-engaged", "all-different", and "all-engaged". In "no-one-engaged", none of the children was engaged with any other and just focused on their own task (e.g. {1, 1, 1}). In "one-less-engaged", one child is less engaged and others are more engaged with each other (e.g. {1, 2, 2}). In "one-more-engaged", one child is more engaged than any other (e.g. {3, 2, 2}). "all-different" means all children have different levels of engagement (e.g. {1, 2, 3}). Lastly, "all-engaged" means that all children are equally engaged without observable differences between them (e.g. {3, 3, 3}). Figure 2 presents each session's proportion of engagement types (the average proportions are $7.1 \pm 4.7\%$, $40.9 \pm 9.1\%$, $7.9 \pm 2.1\%$, 33.3 ± 11.8, and $10.8 \pm 11.7\%$, respectively). Major portions are "one-less-engaged" and "all-different", which means that the children frequently exhibited different levels of engagement. Moreover, we found variations of engagement situations between the groups, which support findings of previous studies [2, 22].

4   Method

In this section, we will present our features: turn-taking and body movement. We will introduce the Ranking SVM algorithm that employs the ordinal annotation scheme. Table 1 summarises all features and their details will be described in the following sections.

Table 1. Feature sets (number of features by functionals) for each child

Category	Features	Functionals
turn-taking (28)	speech (4)	mean-duration
	pause(4)	SD-duration
	speaker change (4)	total-duration
	speaker change with overlap (4)	total-count
	successful interruption (4)	
	unsuccessful interruption (4)	
	overlap (4)	
body (7)	movement (4)	mean-amount
		SD-amount
		total-count
		total-amount
	orientation (1)	mean-orientation
	position x (1)	mean-position
	position y (1)	

4.1   Turn-Taking Features

Based on previous studies [24,27,38], we selected the following turn-taking features: speech, pause, speaker change (change), speaker change with overlap (change.ov), successful interruption (inter), unsuccessful interruption (u.inter), and overlap, as shown in Table 1. More detailed descriptions can be found in [27]. The features were extracted from every 5 s long annotation segment using each child's voice stream. First of all, we extracted each child's speech segments using voice activity detection from each voice stream. Then, to correct errors caused by environmental noise and channel-inferences, we employed iterative speaker identification. Similarly to [12], we used Mel-frequency cepstral coefficients (MFCC) features and the Gaussian-Mixture-Model to detect segments of different speakers. In an iterative way, we updated each speaker's model using the previously extracted segments and manually corrected errors until the models became saturated (no more changes of segments were observed). Finally, we extracted each speaker's speech segments using the saturated models. In real-time applications, on-line speaker segmentation should be applied but we consider this to be future work.

Next, all turn-taking features were extracted from the speech segments detected, and statistical functionals {mean-duration, standard-deviation (SD) of duration, total-duration, and total-count} were applied, as presented in Table 1. Lastly, all values are scaled into the range {0.0–1.0} over each session.

4.2   Body Movement and Segmentation

To extract body movement features, we first performed a foreground segmentation calculating pixel-wise differences between frames, followed by a Gaussian threshold [3]. Next, we identified each child by K-means clustering [3], and extracted movements by using MHI implemented in OpenCV [10,11]. For its robustness, we did not specify which part of body moves (e.g. legs and hands). Instead, we extracted the number (of changes in pixels between frames), orientation, and position (coordinates of x and y) from each movement. Hence, we applied statistical functionals and obtained mean-amount, SD-amount, total-count, total-amount, mean-orientation, and mean-position (x and y) for each child from every annotation segment. As turn-taking features were normalised for each session, all movement features were also scaled into the same range.

4.3   Ranking SVM

As other ranking methods (e.g. ListNet) are suitable if the number of instances in an order is variant [15], Ranking SVM, categorised as pairwise approach, is more effective in our task where the number of children is invariant. To learn an order of engagement between children, we compare only feature vectors of two children in the same constraint. In our task, the constraint is the period of time. In other words, we do not compare children's feature vectors which have different time periods. Therefore, a value of the constraint, often called qid, is each annotation segment's index representing given moments in the range of [0, the total number of segments for each session]. More detailed explanation of Ranking SVM can be found in [23,26].

5   Analysis and Results

Based on our annotation scheme, we extracted all feature values described in Sect. 4. In this section, we present the analysis of our features with respect to engagement levels, the detection experiments and their results.

5.1   Feature Analysis

Since our annotation schemes are ordinal, we looked into differences of feature values between children depending on their ordinal relations of engagement levels. For example, if one child is more engaged than the other child, is this child also more active in speaking or moving? Moreover, we do not have prior knowledge of the proper size of a window for feature extraction in our study. In previous

Table 2. Average of feature values (mean-count) with respect to ordinal relations of engagement levels (**higher**: if the engagement level is higher, **lower**: the engagement level is lower)

Engagement	Speech	Pause	change.ov	inter	u.inter	Overlap	Movement
higher	.242	.233	.198	.080	.052	.139	.187
lower	.178	.164	.164	.068	.042	.115	.168

work [25,29,33], windows of between 0.5 s and 5 min long were used to predict engagement and dominance. To decide an optimal length of windows for detection experiments, we investigated the effect of different window length varying: {5 s, 10 s, 15 s, 20 s, and 25 s}. First, we collected all feature values in the pairwise way for each engagement window (grouped by qid: segment ID) with different lengths. To decide a new engagement level for each window, we utilised a major voting policy. Next, we grouped feature values by ordinal relations: **higher** and **lower**. All features values extracted from children who had higher ranks are categorised into **higher**. Otherwise, feature values are categorised into **lower**. Next, to validate significance of differences between the feature values of **higher** and **lower**, we conducted a Wilcoxon signed-rank test (alternative: greater) that is a non-parametric paired difference test [36].

We found that 20 s long windows produced the largest number (7) of features that have significant differences of both mean-count and mean-amount (or length) between ranks ($p < .0001$). 5s long windows produced the smallest number (4) of features, which means that 5 s long windows are not sufficiently long to capture turn-taking and movement features. Hence, we decided to choose 20 s long windows for subsequent analyses and detection experiments. Table 2 summarises our findings of 20 s long windows. Note that we list only significant results (with $p < .0001$), and present the normalised values of mean-count. Moreover, we analysed feature values of all segments to look at overall characteristics of feature values while cross-validation was employed for evaluation in Sect. 5.2.

Except for speaker change, all turn-taking features showed significant differences. From these findings, we concluded that as some children are more engaged than others at given moments, they tend to show more active turn-taking in conversations. For movement features, amount and count of movement were the most significantly discriminative between higher and lower ranks. Possibly, orientation and positions might not be related with ranks in a linear way.

5.2   Detection Experiments

In this section, we present detection experiments using Ranking SVM. As a baseline, SVM classification (**SVM**) was compared to Ranking SVM (**SVMRANK**). As an exploratory study, we did not select our features using selection methods for ranking [20]. Rather, we compared performances of feature groups: turn-taking and movement. Furthermore, we combined these features at feature level to see if they would complement each other and increase performances in two different situations: **all** and **speech**. **all** includes silent samples while **speech** excludes silent samples. We investigated how much movement features complement turn-taking features in these challenging situations.

For purposes of reproduction, we utilised the implementation of LIBSVM and its extensions [16,30]. Parameters of each model were optimised by a simple grid search. For evaluation, we used the normalised Kendall tau distance, which is a widely used evaluation method for rank learning [18]. To calculate it for two lists (e.g. X_1 and X_2), it is defined as follows:

$$K(X_1, X_2) = \frac{D}{N(N-1)/2} \qquad (1)$$

where D is the total number of swapped pairs and N is the total number of elements in a list. If all orders are incorrect, then it becomes 1.0 while indicating 0.0 for completely correct orders, which can be regarded as an error rate. To test the statistical significance of differences between the methods, we employed a paired corrected t-test [9] (p-values are separately provided with the results).

We look into performances of each feature set using Leave-One-Session-Out-Cross-Validation (LOSOCV). In each fold, one session is used for validation and all other sessions are used for training. Since we have 3 children's samples per segment, a total of 4530 samples (including silent samples 1011) were used and the average number of test samples is 566 and that of training is 3735. Figure 3 summarises two results, all samples (**all**) and samples without silent segments (**speech**).

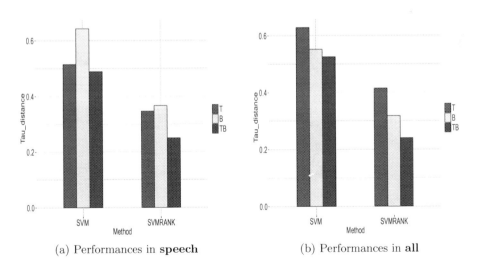

(a) Performances in **speech**   (b) Performances in **all**

Fig. 3. Summary of performances (normalised Kendall tau distance): T (turn-taking), B (body movement), TB (combined)

5.3   Results

First of all, **SVMRANK** outperformed **SVM** with significant differences
($p < .0001$) in both **speech** and **all**. In other words, **SVMRANK** was effective in modelling relative levels of engagement using not only vocal interactions (i.e. turn-taking), but also body movement in the multimodal detection.
In Fig. 3(a) showing cases of **speech**, performances of turn-taking features (T)
were slightly superior to those of body movement features (B). However, the
differences between T and B are not significant ($p = .6$). Second, in cases of
all (see Fig. 3(b)), B outperformed T with significant differences ($p = .0290$).
Although turn-taking features showed discriminative power between higher and
lower ranks in the previous section, they did not show promising results. Since we
conducted neither non-linear correlation analyses nor error analyses of **speech**
and **all**, separately, our findings are not conclusive yet. However, combined features showed the best performances and reduced error rates of both turn-taking
and body movement features with significant levels ($p = .0014$ and $p = 0.0043$,
respectively) for **all**. In other words, turn-taking and body movement features
complemented each other, leading to the best results. In addition, Fig. 4 presents
results of inter-session performances of **all**. As displayed, depending on the
groups of children, the performances fluctuated. While gains of TB with respect
to T and B vary, TB reduced errors for most sessions. In particular, for session
1, TB reduced errors of T by nearly .33. Moreover, TB showed the smallest variation over sessions (.003). In other words, the combined feature set was robust
against inter-group dynamics.

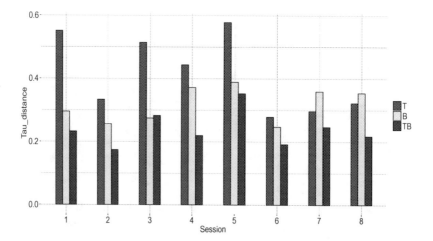

Fig. 4. Intra-session performances: T (turn taking), B (body movement), TB (combined features)

5.4   Limitations and Future Work

While turn-taking features outperformed movement features in **speech**, their performances were degraded in **all** where "silent" moments often occurred. Since the combined features achieved the best performances in both **speech** and **all**, we concluded that turn-taking and movement features complemented each other, which is promising for applications in the wild. However, non-linear relations between features and engagement levels still remain unexplored. Thus, levels of feature or decision fusion should be investigated. For example, we could build separated classifiers for different situations. Furthermore, we might be able to utilise more advanced visual features (e.g. gaze, blinking, gesture) which have semantic information for engagement [1]. While these features were widely used in controlled or laboratory settings [4,6,29], we should investigate rigorous methods to extract these features in naturalistic settings where we cannot regulate children's behaviours.

6   Conclusions

We explored the multimodal engagement detection of individuals using non-verbal features, turn-taking and body movement, in the context of children's collaborative play. To observe spontaneous engagement in groups of three children, we did not impose any restriction on children's conversations and their movements. As a consequence, there were silent situations and limited viewpoints that hindered the automatic extraction of non-verbal features. Moreover, groups of three children exhibited large variations of interactions with temporal dynamics. To address the large variations, we showed that levels of engagement can be characterised by relative levels between children. Moreover, we conducted detection experiments of individual engagement levels using turn-taking and movement features. The Ranking SVM outperformed the SVM classification, which means that the ranking method could be better suited for the multimodal detection of engagement in groups of children. Furthermore, while each feature set alone did not achieve promising results, the combined feature set showed significant error reduction, which means that turn-taking and body movement features complemented each other. As future work, we will conduct more detailed feature analysis including non-linear correlation analysis and investigate methods of integrating our multimodal features.

Acknowledgements. The research leading to these results was supported by the European Community's 7th Framework Programme under Grant agreement 610532 (SQUIRREL - Clearing Clutter Bit by Bit). This work was also partially performed within the Labex SMART (ANR-11-LABX-65) supported by French state funds managed by the ANR within the Investissements dAvenir programme under reference ANR-11-IDEX-0004-02. We would like to thank S.M. Anzalone, S.V. Waveren and F.V. Dixhoorn.

References

1. Aggarwal, J.K., Park, S.: Human motion: modeling and recognition of actions and interactions. In: Proceedings of 2nd International Symposium on 3D Data Processing, Visualization and Transmission, 2004. 3DPVT 2004, pp. 640–647. IEEE (2004)
2. Al Moubayed, S., Lehman, J.: Toward better understanding of engagement in multiparty spoken interaction with children. In: Proceedings of the International Conference on Multimodal Interaction, pp. 211–218. ACM (2015)
3. Antić, B., Letić, D., Crnojević, V., et al.: K-means based segmentation for real-time zenithal people counting. In: Proceedings of International Conference on Image Processing (ICIP), pp. 2565–2568. IEEE (2009)
4. Anzalone, S.M., Boucenna, S., Ivaldi, S., Chetouani, M.: Evaluating the engagement with social robots. Int. J. Soc. Robot. **7**(4), 465–478 (2015)
5. Argyle, M.: Social Interaction, vol. 103. Transaction Publishers (1973)
6. Bianchi-Berthouze, N., Kim, W.W., Patel, D.: Does body movement engage you more in digital game play? and why? In: Paiva, A.C.R., Prada, R., Picard, R.W. (eds.) ACII 2007. LNCS, vol. 4738, pp. 102–113. Springer, Heidelberg (2007). doi:10.1007/978-3-540-74889-2_10
7. Oertel gen bierbach, C.: On the use of multimodal cues for the prediction of involvement in spontaneous conversation. In: Proceedings of the INTERSPEECH, pp. 1541–1544 (2011)
8. Bobick, A.F.: Movement, activity and action: the role of knowledge in the perception of motion. Philos. Trans. R. Soc. Lond. B Biol. Sci. **352**(1358), 1257–1265 (1997)
9. Bouckaert, R.R., Frank, E.: Evaluating the replicability of significance tests for comparing learning algorithms. In: Dai, H., Srikant, R., Zhang, C. (eds.) PAKDD 2004. LNCS (LNAI), vol. 3056, pp. 3–12. Springer, Heidelberg (2004). doi:10.1007/978-3-540-24775-3_3
10. Bradski, G., Kaehler, A.: Learning OpenCV: Computer Vision with the OpenCV Library. O'Reilly Media Inc., Sebastopol (2008)
11. Bradski, G.R., Davis, J.W.: Motion segmentation and pose recognition with motion history gradients. Mach. Vis. Appl. **13**(3), 174–184 (2002)
12. Busso, C., Georgiou, G., P., Narayanan, S.S.: Real-time monitoring of participant's interaction in a meeting using audio-visual sensors. In: Proceedings of the IEEE International Conference on Acoustics, Speech and Signal Processing (ICASSP). IEEE (2007)
13. Campbell, N., Scherer, S.: Comparing measures of synchrony and alignment in dialogue speech timing with respect to turn-taking activity. In: Proceedings of the INTERSPEECH, pp. 2546–2549 (2010)
14. Cao, H., Verma, R., Nenkova, A.: Speaker-sensitive emotion recognition via ranking: studies on acted and spontaneous speech. Comput. Speech Lang. **29**(1), 186–202 (2015)
15. Cao, Z., Qin, T., Liu, T.Y., Tsai, M.F., Li, H.: Learning to rank: from pairwise approach to listwise approach. In: Proceedings of International Conference on Machine Learning, pp. 129–136. ACM (2007)
16. Chang, C.C., Lin, C.J.: LIBSVM: a library for support vector machines. ACM Trans. Intell. Syst. Technol. (TIST) **2**(3), 27 (2011)
17. Dittmann, A.T., Llewellyn, L.G.: Body movement and speech rhythm in social conversation. J. Personal. Soc. Psychol. **11**(2), 98 (1969)

18. Fagin, R., Kumar, R., Sivakumar, D.: Comparing top k lists. SIAM J. Discrete Math. **17**(1), 134–160 (2003)
19. Gatica-Perez, D., McCowan, I.A., Zhang, D., Bengio, S.: Detecting group interest-level in meetings. Technical report, IDIAP (2004)
20. Geng, X., Liu, T.Y., Qin, T., Li, H.: Feature selection for ranking. In: Proceedings of the International Conference on Research and Development in Information Retrieval, pp. 407–414. ACM (2007)
21. Gupta, R., Lee, C.c., Lee, S., Narayanan, S.: Assessment of a child's engagement using sequence model based features. In: Workshop on Affective Social Speech Signals (2013)
22. Hall, J.A., Coats, E.J., LeBeau, L.S.: Nonverbal behavior and the vertical dimension of social relations: a meta-analysis. Psychol. Bull. **131**(6), 898 (2005)
23. Hang, L.: A short introduction to learning to rank. IEICE Trans. Inf. Syst. **94**(10), 1854–1862 (2011)
24. Heldner, M., Edlund, J.: Pauses, gaps and overlaps in conversations. J. Phon. **38**(4), 555–568 (2010)
25. Jayagopi, D.B., Ba, S., Odobez, J.M., Gatica-Perez, D.: Predicting two facets of social verticality in meetings from five-minute time slices and nonverbal cues. In: Proceedings of International Conference on Multimodal Interfaces, pp. 45–52. ACM (2008)
26. Joachims, T.: Optimizing search engines using clickthrough data. In: Proceedings of the International Conference on Knowledge Discovery and Data Mining, pp. 133–142. ACM (2002)
27. Kim, J., Truong, K.P., Charisi, V., Zaga, C., Lohse, M., Heylen, D., Evers, V.: Vocal turn-taking patterns in groups of children performing collaborative tasks: an exploratory study. In: Proceedings of the INTERSPEECH, pp. 1645–1649 (2015)
28. Kim, J., Truong, K.P., Evers, V.: Automatic detection of children's engagement using non-verbal features and ordinal learning. In: Workshop on Child Computer Interaction (2016)
29. Leite, I., McCoy, M., Ullman, D., Salomons, N., Scassellati, B.: Comparing models of disengagement in individual and group interactions. In: Proceedings of Annual ACM/IEEE International Conference on Human-Robot Interaction, pp. 99–105. ACM (2015)
30. Li, L., Lin, H.T.: Ordinal regression by extended binary classification. In: Advances in Neural Information Processing Systems, pp. 865–872 (2006)
31. Parten, M.B.: Social participation among pre-school children. J. Abnorm. Soc. Psychol. **27**(3), 243 (1932)
32. Piaget, J.: The Psychology of the Child. Basic Books, New York (1972)
33. Pianesi, F., Zancanaro, M., Lepri, B., Cappelletti, A.: A multimodal annotated corpus of consensus decision making meetings. Lang. Resour. Eval. **41**(3–4), 409–429 (2007)
34. Robins, B., Dautenhahn, K., Te Boekhorst, R., Billard, A.: Robotic assistants in therapy and education of children with autism: can a small humanoid robot help encourage social interaction skills? Univers. Access Inf. Soc. **4**(2), 105–120 (2005)
35. Sidner, C.L., Lee, C., Kidd, C.D., Lesh, N., Rich, C.: Explorations in engagement for humans and robots. Artif. Intell. **166**(1), 140–164 (2005)
36. Siegel, S.: Nonparametric Statistics for the Behavioral Sciences. McGraw-Hill, New York (1956)
37. Stangor, C.: Social Groups in Action and Interaction. Psychology Press, New York (2004)

38. Vinciarelli, A., Pantic, M., Heylen, D., Pelachaud, C., Poggi, I., D'Errico, F., Schröder, M.: Bridging the gap between social animal and unsocial machine: a survey of social signal processing. IEEE Trans. Affect. Comput. **3**(1), 69–87 (2012)
39. Wittenburg, P., Brugman, H., Russel, A., Klassmann, A., Sloetjes, H.: ELAN: a professional framework for multimodality research. In: Proceedings of LREC, pp. 5–8 (2006)

Daily Behaviors

Anomaly Detection in Elderly Daily Behavior in Ambient Sensing Environments

Oya Aran[1(✉)], Dairazalia Sanchez-Cortes[1], Minh-Tri Do[1],
and Daniel Gatica-Perez[1,2]

[1] Idiap Research Institute, Martigny, Switzerland
{oaran,dscortes,gatica}@idiap.ch, minhtrido@gmail.com
[2] Ecole Polytechnique Federale de Lausanne (EPFL), Lausanne, Switzerland

Abstract. Current ubiquitous computing applications for smart homes aim to enhance people's daily living respecting age span. Among the target groups of people, elderly are a population eager for "choices for living arrangements", which would allow them to continue living in their homes but at the same time provide the health care they need. Given the growing elderly population, there is a need for statistical models able to capture the recurring patterns of daily activity life and reason based on this information. We present an analysis of real-life sensor data collected from 40 different households of elderly people, using motion, door and pressure sensors. Our objective is to automatically observe and model the daily behavior of the elderly and detect anomalies that could occur in the sensor data. For this purpose, we first introduce an abstraction layer to create a common ground for home sensor configurations. Next, we build a probabilistic spatio-temporal model to summarize daily behavior. Anomalies are then defined as significant changes from the learned behavioral model and detected using a cross-entropy measure. We have compared the detected anomalies with manually collected annotations and the results show that the presented approach is able to detect significant behavioral changes of the elderly.

Keywords: Anomaly detection · Healthcare · Elderly care · Sensor networks

1 Introduction

Pervasive and ubiquitous computing is essential to understand human behavior. Multimodal and more seamless embedded sensors support advances in human behavior understanding, covering a diversity of challenging topics including personality, emotions, human mobility and activities in everyday life [5,8,9,14,22]. The learned lessons make room to implement convenient applications aiming to enhance day to day living of people through their different age span.

The elderly constitute a group that deserves special attention to support their daily life [3]. Previous research has shown that seniors want to have choices

---

Do is currently affiliated with Gameloft, Ho Chi Minh City, Vietnam.

© Springer International Publishing AG 2016
M. Chetouani et al. (Eds.): HBU 2016, LNCS 9997, pp. 51–67, 2016.
DOI: 10.1007/978-3-319-46843-3_4

for their living arrangements, i.e., preserving as long as possible their sense of personal space, independence and autonomy [6,30]. While nursing homes are a standing option, they have a great risk of overpopulation in the coming years [3] and in addition it may not be the ideal option for people who prefer to live independently. A good alternative is to consider converting traditional homes into low-cost smart homes. A comprehensive survey on such systems can be found in [4], which also discusses the design considerations like unobtrusiveness, scalability, energy efficiency, and security.

The smart home concept includes homes embedded with simple environmental sensors and more complex systems including audio, video and biometric systems. Systems that are easy to put in place, that do not demand maintenance from the user and are affordable in terms of cost, give elderly and their families the option to age at home while being monitored. There is evidence that opportunistic home surveillance prevents in some cases hospitalization [20]. While there are several significant advances on activity recognition in smart homes for elderly [10,12,23,31], relatively few studies tackle the challenging topic of detecting "unusual" behavior on elderly [13,21,25,28]. In most of these studies, experiments are performed monitoring either non-elderly subjects or very few elderly subjects, thus the proposed frameworks are not necessarily generalizable. Overall findings reveal that there is a compromise between high accuracy on anomalous behavior detection and subjects' privacy.

The raw information captured by the sensors can not be shared as such with the medical staff or used directly to detect changes in behavior automatically. Statistical models are needed to capture recurring patterns of daily life activities. This extracted knowledge about recurring patterns could be used to enrich the information displayed to the medical staff and improve the precision of early detections.

In this paper, we present a framework to analyze elderly daily behavior using only motion and state-change sensors. As an almost seamless and unobtrusive setting, it provides a promising approach for adoption among elderly and has shown to sufficiently capture day to day activities in real settings. The analysis used in this study is based on data gathered from 40 elderly homes on a four month period. In addition to the sensor data, there are annotations from questionnaires and daily activity journals. Our contributions in this paper can be summarized as follows.

1. We propose to use an abstraction layer, with the purpose of creating a common ground for different possible sensor configurations and sensor types. Given the high variability in the type, the number and the position of the sensors in different apartments, the abstraction layer enables an approach that could be generalized to different home environments and multiple datasets.
2. Based on the location and outing inferences on the abstraction layer, we propose a probabilistic behavior model to summarize daily activities of subjects from their sensor activation data. The probabilistic model takes into account the location of the subject at each hour of the day and defines a likelihood of the subject's behavior based on her/his location and outings.

This model, computed over a long period of sensor data, indicates where the subject spends her/his time as part of a daily routine.

3. We show that the presented behavior model can be used to detect anomalies by comparing the actual behavioral data of a subject with her/his usual behavior, as modeled by the behavior model. We follow an unsupervised approach and use a cross-entropy measure to indicate the predictability of the data, which is used as the anomaly indicator score. To detect whether there is an anomaly at a given time, the score is thresholded to obtain the anomaly detections.

In the next section, we present the related work in the literature. Section 3 presents our approach, the sensing environment, and the data used in this study. In Sects. 4, 5 and 6, we present our contributions on the sensor abstraction layer, the user behavioral model, and the anomaly detection. Section 7 provides discussion and conclusions.

2   Related Work

The use of pervasive computing devices has recently supported advances in understanding personality, preferences, emotions, human mobility and daily activity routines from longitudinal data [5,8,9,14,22]. A significant population that would benefit from accurate inferences and clear understanding of daily activity routines is the elderly population. Systems able to provide opportunistic information to relatives or healthcare professionals in charge of elderly, would provide more confidence to elderly living independently.

In the context of smart home research, there have been centered efforts in inferring Activities of Daily Living (ADL) with state-of-the-art machine techniques using manually annotated data. Noury et al. [24] presented an attempt to analyse ADL using an elderly hospital environment. The scenario included a hospital suite embedded with infrared sensors used to record daily activity of an elderly woman for a two-month period. Their findings reported significant correlations between diurnal and nocturnal activities in elderly. Moreover, Hong and Nugent [15] reported 83.4 % overall activity accuracy on seven daily activities. For the study, a three room apartment was equipped with 14 state-change sensors. The reported performance corresponds to a 28 days observational period from a 26 year old male.

More recently, [29] reported 91.3 % accuracy inferring eight daily activities. A couple of subject houses were equipped with 10 wireless sensors (5 including ambient). The activity observations corresponded to 20 consecutive days of 10 healthy subjects (6 women, 4 men) between 28 and 79 years old. The activities were annotated by the subjects with pen and paper, and also with a wireless device. Similarly, Pereira et al. reported up to 83 % accuracy recognizing 7 typical movement activities. The framework combine sensing from wearable, portable and environmental sensors [27]. The movement activities were collected from 10 volunteers aged between 19 and 51, and later on manually annotated. Fleury et al. [10] reported 13.7 % global error rate on seven inferred activities.

For the study, an in-lab smart home was equipped with six infrared sensors, four door contacts, one temperature sensor, eight microphones, 5 webcameras and a wearable kinematic sensor. Although results presented in [10] look promising, the design of the scenario including audio and visual sensors might not be in harmony with common elderly expectations regarding non-intrusive and privacy protection sensors at home.

It is worth to note that above cited works do not take under consideration the problem of anomaly detection. Anomaly detection *"refers to the problem of finding patterns in data that do not conform to expected behavior"* [7]. This topic is highly relevant in the context of ADL and sensor data in smart homes [17, 18, 21], and should be considered as critical for the deployment of elderly surveillance systems [16].

A Bayesian formulation is provided for anomaly detection in [26]. Behavioral patterns of the residents were extracted using Bayesian statistics, based on the raw measures of user activity, captured by several event-based sensors. The behavior was statistically estimated based on three probabilistic features: sensor activation likelihood, sensor sequence likelihood, and sensor event duration likelihood. The validation of the results has been performed on a data collected from three different home settings, with adult or elderly subjects living alone. The data is collected for 14 to 25 days.

Kim and Chung presented in [19] a framework that serves to monitor emergency situations of patients with chronic diseases. The framework proposes the use of wearable devices (including GPS), ambient and motion sensors as well as video cameras and speakers. The emergency module follows a rule-based semantic inference which outputs a list of actions to be taken. The module relies on the motion history image and continuous tracking.

The research in [28] proposes to compute a wellness index to capture abnormal behavior using several weeks of observations from elderly living alone. For the study, 6 wireless sensors (active/inactive) were installed in four elderly houses during several weeks. Nine ADL are inferred [28] from the embedded sensors and the wellness function aims to capture how "healthy" is the elderly person, i.e., being able to perform daily activities. The wellness function estimates maximum and minimum thresholds for the given activities computed after a trial run period of one week. After the trial period, warning messages are generated whenever wellness values passed the thresholds. More recently, [11] approached the inference of abnormalities and detection of changes in routine behavior. For the study, three months data of 10 users was synthetically generated, the data consisting of vital signs (heart rate, blood pressure, blood sugar, respiration and temperature), location, activity and lifestyle. With 8 activities, the accuracy of activity sequence is estimated above 87 % with normal observations and above 90 % with abnormal observations. After the abnormalities are detected, they propose a method that uses fuzzy rules to describe actions to be taken.

In the above studies, the following observations can be made on the data used for the analysis.

– The data comes from few households: It is challenging to install sensors on different households. However, it is also challenging to analyze data coming from multiple households, in which there are different sensor configurations due to different floor plans, number of rooms, etc. In this paper, we propose to use an abstraction layer, which allows us to analyze the data coming from different sensor configurations. The data that we analyze come from 40 different households.

– The data is collected from non-elderly people: It is a challenging task to collect data from elderly people due to privacy and technology adoption reasons. Due to this, most studies use data coming from adults and young adults. In our study, we use data coming from subjects aged 62 to 96, with an average age of 84, spanning a truly elderly population.

– The data hardly contains ground-truth labels: Annotating daily routine behavior is cumbersome. In particular for elderly people, they have troubles remembering to annotate during their daily routines and have to use the classical pen and paper interface for the annotations as they do not always cope well with technological devices such as smart phones or tablets. These factors limit the amount of ground truth labels that can be obtained. In our study, we are also limited by the amount of available annotations. We use manual annotations of ADL coming from one of the subjects, spanning 8 days.

3   Our Approach

The overall objective of this study is to analyze daily routine behavior of elderly people in their apartment through ambient sensors. In particular, we aim to detect anomalies and significant changes in the behavior, with the assumption that these anomalies may signal health related problems. In the next sections, we present the sensing environment and the details of the dataset that has been used in the study.

3.1   Sensing Environment

We have used data coming from a commercial product, which includes ambient sensors installed in apartments where elderly live [1]. The product enables the caregivers to monitor the patients' activity and daily behavior based on the sensor data. The sensor system includes a base unit and wireless, battery-powered sensors which are installed in strategic locations around the apartment. The sensors include open/close door (for main entrance and fridge), force sensors (for bed and chair), motion/activity sensors in the living room, bedroom, etc., and smoke sensors.

3.2   Dataset

The data used for experiments was collected in the context of a Swiss project from mid-December 2013 to early April 2014. The data collection was led by

DomoSafety [1] and La Source, School of Nursing Sciences, University of Applied Sciences of Western Switzerland [2]. The collected data includes 45 unique subjects, covering a total of 104 days. During this period, some of the subjects dropped out from the data collection due to various reasons. For further analysis and to maintain consistency among the available recorded dates, five subjects were discarded from the study. All data used in the paper was handled in an anonymized way.

The recruitment of the subjects lasted a couple of months before the start of the data collection. For each recruited subject, an initial questionnaire was applied at the time of the recruitment, prior to the data collection. The average age of the subjects is 84.3 years, with a minimum age of 62 years and a maximum of 96. The 40 subjects in the study comprise 27 females and 13 males.

Regarding external help for daily living, 31 subjects declared receiving professional cleaning services, 25 using food delivery services, and 28 subjects declared receiving help from family. 25 subjects reported climbing stairs without help. 35 subjects declared having regular outings. 29 subjects declared to be widow/er, 3 married, 4 single and 2 divorced. Other questions also captured general health problems, such as medicines taken, nutritional status, overall physical and functional state.

Sensor Data. The original data comprises several measurements at different frame rates from various types of sensors. The number, types, and location of sensors vary for each installation depending on the configuration of the corresponding apartment. Figure 1 shows an example configuration of the analyzed static sensors from one subject's apartment.

Journal Annotations. With the aim of having a source of ground truth, the collection includes daily activity journal (DAJ) annotations that has been performed twice during the study. A first set of annotations was collected at the start of the study from three subjects, with the purpose of evaluating the newly installed sensors. A second and a more reliable set of annotations was collected from a single subject towards the end of the data collection. The resident was

Fig. 1. Floor plan with static sensors from one subject's apartment.

asked to report the start and end time of the following activities: *bathroom visits*, *meals*, *visits*, and *outings*. To make the annotation task easier for the subjects, the diaries were split based on activities performed in each location, printed in paper, and placed accordingly in the apartment.

4   Sensor Data Abstraction Layer

The sensor network used in our study continuously captures a set of measurements at different frame rates from various types of sensors. The number, types, and location of these sensors vary in different installations depending on the configuration of the corresponding apartment. For instance, a two-room apartment will be equipped with less sensors than a five-room one. A large living room requires more than one activity sensor to cover its volume.

We built an abstraction layer to overcome the variability of the sensor configuration. This abstraction layer takes all the sensor values as input and generates sequences of *events* as output. An *event* is simply defined by its respective start and end timestamps and a label. We consider two event types in this study: **Locations** and **Outings**.

This abstraction layer produces a new representation of the data that simplifies the raw sensor measurements and allows the system to be independent of the number and types of sensors found in an apartment. In the next sections, we describe the modules which extract abstract events from the raw sensor data. We then evaluate its performance by comparing the sequences of events estimated by the abstraction layer to a written diary that serves as ground truth (see Sect. 4.3).

4.1   Location Inference

In the study, the sensors are installed in different positions of the apartment. When a sensor fires, the location of the resident is registered. We developed an algorithm that makes use of the localized activity signals to infer the actual location of the resident. Given the activity signals, the algorithm outputs a sequence of location events, consisting of the start time, end time, and the location label.

The algorithm keeps track of the location by examining the set of incoming signals and updates the location state accordingly. We assume that the resident does not change the location when no activity has been detected. In other words, the location is updated only if one or several activity signals occur. In practice, we can guarantee this assumption by installing the sensors at key locations, to make sure that the system can detect activity whenever the resident enters a new location.

At a given time, if there is exactly one activity signal, the location update is straightforward. However, it might happen that multiple signals arrive at the same time, and that these signals do not come from the same location. This issue occurs when the coverage area of different sensors are overlapping (e.g., a sensor inside the bathroom and a sensor in front of the bathroom door can

---

Algorithm 1. Location Inference

1: Input: activity signals $\mathbf{s} = (s_i.time, s_i.location)_{i=1..n}$, location set $\mathcal{L}$
2: Output: sequence of location events $\mathbf{l} = (l_i.start, l_i.end, l_i.location)_{i=1..m}$
3: Method: update location $\mathbf{l}$ based on the duration of the activity signals, $\mathbf{s}$

Algorithm 2. Outing classification

1: Input: raw signals $\mathbf{s}$, indices of two consecutive entrance door signals k, h
2: Output: Indicate if the period $(s_k.time, s_h.time)$ corresponds to an outing
3: Method: Classify as outing if there are no activities in between two consecutive entrance door signals k, h

---

both detect activity when the resident enters the bathroom) or when the sensors are not perfectly synchronized. In this situation, the algorithm needs to choose one location among several candidates. Algorithm 1 shows the summary of the location inference algorithm.

4.2 Outing Detection

To analyze the subject's behavior and make sense of sensor data, it is important to know whether the subject is inside the apartment. In this section, we present an algorithm to infer outing events by using information from the entrance door and the activity in the apartment. The door openings provide potential outing event candidates, which are then verified by checking if there is any activity inside the apartment during the period of interest.

We assume that the resident always closes the door after leaving the apartment and opens the entrance door to enter the apartment. This assumption simplifies the problem as we only need to check if a period between two consecutive door signals is actually an outing. The outing classification decision is made after verifying that there are no activities inside the apartment between two consecutive door signals. Algorithm 2 shows the summary of the outing classification algorithm.

4.3 Evaluation

We evaluate the quality of the outputs of the abstraction layer with a daily activity journal (DAJ) filled by one subject for 8 consecutive days. We use the bathroom and outing annotations from the DAJ as ground truth data to evaluate the performance of the abstraction layer on predicting the bathroom visits and outings events.

To analyze the sensor data, we split the time scale in five-minute segments and consider each segment as the basic unit in our evaluation. For each of the events we consider (outings and bathroom usage), both for the journal annotations and sensor data, if there is any reported event within a given segment, that segment is labeled as true for the corresponding event. For the evaluation, from these time-aligned binary values, we compute the confusion matrix between two systems: the ground truth values coming from the journal annotations and the sensor values. We consider the journal annotations as the reference.

Location: To evaluate location inference, we focus on the bathroom events, as we have ground truth annotations for the bathroom usage. The abstraction layer provides a sequence of bathroom events that we compare to the DAJ ground truth data. A total of 52 bathroom visits have been reported by the resident, which corresponds to 94 segments of 5 min. 13 segments have been wrongly labeled as non-bathroom events by the system, and 46 segments have been wrongly labeled as bathroom visits. This corresponds to a precision of 64 % and a recall of 86 % for the bathroom usage. Table 1(a) shows the confusion matrix for the bathroom events.

Outings: We correctly predict 245 segments (20.4 h) out of 21.8 h of outings reported in the diary. A total of 39 segments (3.25 h) are wrongly assigned to outings. Table 1(b) shows the confusion matrix for the outing events. The precision is 86 % and the recall is 94 %.

Table 1. Abstraction layer evaluation based on the comparison of the diary ground truth data and the sensor data. (a) Confusion matrix of the bathroom usage events, and (b) Confusion matrix of the outing events.

(a)

	Sensor-False	Sensor-True
Journal-False	2164 (TN)	46 (FP)
Journal-True	13 (FN)	81 (TP)

(b)

	Sensor-False	Sensor-True
Journal-False	2003 (TN)	39 (FP)
Journal-True	17 (FN)	245 (TP)

5 User Behavioral Model

5.1 Location Based Probabilistic Model

We introduce a statistical model for summarizing behavioral data of a subject. For each subject, we assume that the location at a given timestamp depends only on the hour of the day. Let $\mathbf{l} = \{l_t\}$ be the location sequence and $\mathbf{h} = \{h_t\}$ denotes the sequence of hour-of-the-day where $h_t \in \{1..24\}$. The likelihood of the data can be defined as follows:

$$p(\mathbf{l}; \mathbf{h}, \theta) = \prod_h \prod_l \theta_{h,l}^{n(l,h,\mathbf{l},\mathbf{h})}$$

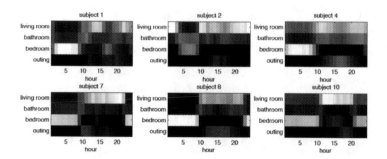

Fig. 2. Samples of user behavioral model. Brightness of each cell represents the conditional probability of being at a location at a given hour.

where $\theta_{h,l} = P(l|h)$ denote the probability of being at location l at *hour* h, $n(l, h, \mathbf{l}, \mathbf{h}) = \sum_i \mathbb{1}(l_i = l \wedge h_i = h)$ is the count of location l in time slot h. Note that we treat $\mathbf{h}$ as external information instead of the observation in the probabilistic model.

Let $(\mathbf{l}_s, \mathbf{h}_s)$ be the data for subject s, the parameter of the categorical distribution is computed as follows:

$$\theta_{h,l}^{(s)} = \frac{n(l, h, \mathbf{l}_s, \mathbf{h}_s) + \alpha}{\sum_l n(l, h, \mathbf{l}_s, \mathbf{h}_s) + \alpha}$$

where the scalar $\alpha > 0$ is introduced for the regularization purposes. In our experiment, we see that the results do not change significantly with respect to α, thus we set $\alpha = 1$.

Figure 2 illustrates different samples of behavioral model, which summarize daily activities of different subjects. For each hour of the day, we use a discrete distribution over the four location categories to characterize the mobility pattern of the subject.

5.2   Discovering Common Behavioral Patterns

The model reveals several behavioral patterns such as the going to bed time, waking up time, or sleep interruptions during the night. As an analysis of the common behavioral patterns shared by different subjects, we applied clustering on the behavioral profiles of different users. We used k-means clustering with two clusters. For each subject, we concatenated values of the behavioral patterns of that subject into a vector, forming a feature vector of size 96 (24 h × 4 locations). Figure 3 shows the mean profiles in each cluster. We see that there are two typical behaviors among the participants of the study. A majority of the subjects spend their time in the living room and sleep in their bedroom at night, with occasional outings and several bathroom visits during the day (Fig. 3, right). However, the other group of subjects does not seem to use their bedroom for their night sleep (Fig. 3, left). This is an important observation, as it has implications particularly on the placement of the sensors, i.e. the bed sensor.

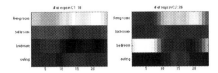

Fig. 3. Mean behavior profiles for two clusters.

6 Anomaly Indicator

We define anomalies as events, which are different than the subjects' past behavior, as modeled by the behavior model defined in Sect. 5. There can be several reasons for anomalies, ranging from sensor failures to particular health problems that the patient might have. Accurate and timely detection of anomalies are highly informative for the caregivers and can be life saving in particular situations.

6.1 Measuring the Data Predictability

We assume that any anomaly can be measured as deviations from the routine behavior and define a cross-entropy measure as an indicator for the predictability of the data. Given the data $\mathbf{l}, \mathbf{h}$ and the learned behavioral model θ, the cross-entropy is computed as follows:

$$H(\mathbf{l}, \theta; \mathbf{h}) = -\sum_{t=1..T} \frac{1}{T} log_2 p(l_t|\theta, h_t) = -\sum_{t=1..T} \frac{1}{T} log_2 \theta_{h_t, l_t} \tag{1}$$

The cross-entropy measures the average number of bits to encode the data given the learned behavioral model. A low entropy indicates that the empirical distribution is well predicted by the learned model, while a high entropy indicates that the model does not accurately predict the data.

To simulate an online setting, we divide the data of each subject into one-week periods. At the ith week, we learn the model from the behavioral data of the $(i-1)$ previous weeks, and estimate the cross-entropy for each hour and each day of the ith week. Figure 4 illustrates a few samples of our predictability indicator based on cross-entropy. The first line shows the anomaly scores estimated per hour of the day. The second line shows the scores estimated per day. The third line shows the mobility pattern of the subjects including the locations inside the apartment and the outings. Note that for the first week, the training data is empty and uniform distribution is used by default. In many cases, the predictability increases quickly after a few weeks if the daily behavioral data is repetitive, until there are some anomaly in mobility pattern. For example, the plot of subject 8 shows that the first month of data is highly predictable. Then, the fact that the mobility pattern has changed as less repetitive (outing several hours depending on the day) is reflected by the increase in the number of bits needed to encode the new data. Using a shorter temporal resolution, as for the per hour of the day estimation, allows for more rapid estimations. It can be seen that the changes in the behavioral patterns are captured as quickly as possible, immediately following the pattern change, allowing for a shorter response time.

Overall, we can visually find a correlation between the anomaly indicator and the change in mobility behavioral data. This means that the proposed indicator can be potentially used for anomaly detection, with an appropriate threshold value. In the next section, we investigate and compare the accuracy of anomaly detection per day and per hour of the day, when used with different thresholds.

6.2   Anomaly Detection Evaluation

For the validation of the anomaly detector, we need ground truth values that indicate various types of anomalies that could occur. One type of anomaly could be due to sensor malfunction. Either a sensor stops responding or starts providing faulty readings. For example, in Fig. 4, for each subject, there are one or more days, where the subject's location is always recorded as bedroom (green lines), which most probably reflects sensor failures. However, the sensor failures in this dataset have not been logged, thus we do not have access to that information. Another type of anomaly could be due to a significant change in the behavior of the subject, which could signal a health related condition. For example, the subject starts spending more and more time in bed, showing a decrease in the number of outings or the use of the kitchen, etc. If available, subject's health information could also be used as ground truth, in case the person had any important health conditions. Unfortunately, in the dataset used for this study, such information does not exist. To compensate for the lack of ground truth, we have collected manual annotations of anomalies. The location mappings of

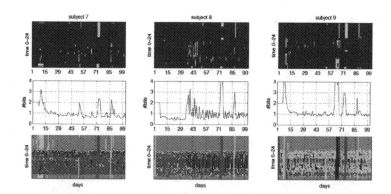

Fig. 4. Anomaly scores on three sample subjects. The figures in the first, second and third rows correspond to scores per hour of the day, scores per day, and the mobility pattern, respectively. For the per hour of the day results in the first row, the anomaly score increases from dark blue to dark red. For the mobility pattern, blue corresponds to living room, green corresponds to bathroom, orange corresponds to bedroom, and red corresponds to outings. (Color figure online)

the subjects is shown to the annotators (i.e. such as the ones in the third row of Fig. 4) and based on this information the annotators indicated the days that they think could be an anomaly. The manual annotations indicate only the day of the anomaly as we decided that any shorter duration could have been harder and unreliable to manually annotate with the information shown during annotation.

The comparison of the anomaly detections with the manual annotations is done as follows:

- The detected anomaly scores are thresholded with a set threshold.
- The hourly detections has been mapped such that if there is an anomaly score higher than the threshold in any hour of the day, that day is considered as an anomaly.
- If a detected anomaly is on the same day as one of the manually annotated anomalies, it is considered as a correct detection, otherwise it is considered as a false detection.

The evaluation is done on a sub-dataset to filter out missing data and considering only subjects who live alone. The final dataset used in the evaluation corresponds to 104 days from 36 subjects. Figure 5 shows the Receiver Operating Characteristic (ROC) curves for anomaly detection. We have used the quantile values to set a threshold and the figure shows the ROC curves drawn with thresholds correspond to the quantile of the data in the range of [0.10–0.995]. We observe that the two approaches give similar results, with the hourly detection giving slightly better results at the threshold levels determined by 0.975 and 0.95 quantile. For a threshold on the 0.95 quantile of anomaly scores detected every hour of the day, the true positive rate is 0.66 and the false positive rate is 0.29. Using per day detection, 0.72 true positive rate can be obtained with

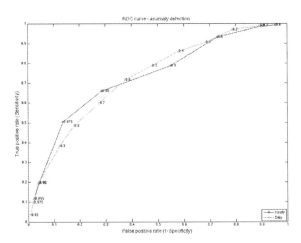

Fig. 5. ROC curves for anomaly detection for two different approaches, per day and per hour of the day. The quantile values used to determine the thresholds are shown next to each data point.

a higher false positive rate, 0.38, based on a threshold determined by the 0.60 quantile of the data.

In addition to the performance measures, the hourly detection has the advantage of reporting the anomaly earlier, at the latest one hour after the anomaly whereas the daily detection needs to wait until the end of the day. From this perspective, shorter temporal resolutions are preferable over the longer ones given similar performance.

7   Discussion and Conclusion

We presented an analysis of real-life sensor data collected from a large number of households with elderly subjects. Our framework first defines an abstract layer to create a common ground for different sensor configurations. We aim to build a behavior model, which represents the subjects' daily behavior based on the events extracted from the abstraction layer. Based on the location and outings events in the abstract layer, our probabilistic behavior model captures the repetitive daily routines of the subjects. The use of an abstraction layer facilitates to generalize the sensor information in terms of events. Thus, the created events are independent of the sensor configuration and type, and summarize the activity of the subjects. For example, in order to detect the living room location in a big apartment, it may be necessary to install two sensors in the living room in order to cover the whole space, whereas in a small apartment, one sensor would be enough. When converted to events, regardless of the number of sensors in the living room, there will be one single event of being in the living room. This generalization allows us to use the same approach in different households with different configurations. While our framework is general, we focus on building a model of location data, which are considered as key in many ubiquitous applications. However, the abstraction approach is not limited to locations and outings but can also be formulated for activity level, event sequence, etc., which would provide additional information to model the subject's behavior. The integration of other data types can be theoretically done by adding more variables to the system.

Once the behavior model is created, we use this model to detect anomalies. We propose an indicator of predictability based on the cross-entropy measure for the detection of anomalies. Our method compares the new observed behavioral data with the learned distribution to measure how well the learned behavioral model predicts the new data. By using cross-entropy, we define the anomaly indicator as the average number of bits to encode the new data. This normalized measurement facilitates the comparison between data periods, subjects, and also future behavior models with additional data types.

One of the assumptions that we used is that there is only one subject in the apartment. Having this assumption, any visitors in the apartment could be detected as an anomaly, unless they are regular visitors. The regular visitors, such as the cleaning person, who come at fixed times in a week and following a similar routine in the apartment, could be captured by the behavior model.

However, this has not been confirmed in the current study as we did not have any accurate information on the visitors of the subjects.

The overall aim in anomaly detection is to detect any type of anomaly and inform the caregivers about the anomaly as soon as it is detected. If it is a sensor anomaly, the sensor needs to be changed as soon as possible. If it is a change in the daily routine of the subject, a visit by the caregiver would be necessary. If it is a sudden and persistent change, it may be an emergency situation. In this study, we only looked at the detection of anomalies without investigating the type of anomaly. To further validate the performance of the anomaly detection, there is a need to gather real-life ground truth labels that indicate different types of anomalies, in particular, the health related ones. The availability of ground truth information for different type of anomalies would also enable us to develop methods that could identify the type of anomaly at the time of detection, which we leave as part of future work. It is also important to note that the detection should be as accurate as possible so that the caregivers are provided with precise information. The accuracy of anomaly detection is dependent on the detection approach as well as the behavior model, which are both based on the sensor data and the abstraction layer. We observe that most of the errors stem from faulty sensor data or wrong sensor placement. Improving sensor quality and a more careful placement of sensors will automatically lead to higher accuracy.

Acknowledgments. This work has been funded by the Swiss Commission for Technology and Innovation (CTI) through the Domocare and Swisko projects. The data used in this study was collected in the context of the Domocare project. The data collection was led by DomoSafety, Switzerland (Guillaume DuPasquier, Edouard Goupy, and Hieu Pham) and La Source, School of Nursing Sciences, University of Applied Sciences of Western Switzerland (Henk Verloo and Christine Cohen.) We would also like to thank Hieu Pham (DomoSafety) and Florent Monay (Idiap) for technical discussions.

References

1. DomoSafety. http://www.domo-safety.com/
2. Institut et Haute Ecole de la Sante La Source. http://www.ecolelasource.ch
3. United Nations, Population Division. http://www.un.org/esa/population/publications/worldageing19502050/pdf/80chapterii.pdf
4. Alemdar, H., Ersoy, C.: Wireless sensor networks for healthcare: a survey. Comput. Netw. **54**(15), 2688–2710 (2010)
5. Alshamsi, A., Pianesi, F., Lepri, B., Pentland, A., Rahwan, I.: Network diversity and affect dynamics: the role of personality traits. PLoS ONE **11**(4), e0152358 (2016)
6. Borsch-Supan, A., Hajivassiliou, V., Kotlikoff, L.J.: Health, children, and elderly living arrangements: a multiperiod-multinomial probit model with unobserved heterogeneity and autocorrelated errors. In: Topics in the Economics of Aging, pp. 79–108. University of Chicago Press (1992)
7. Chandola, V., Banerjee, A., Kumar, V.: Anomaly detection: a survey. ACM Comput. Surv. **41**(3), 15:1–15:58 (2009). http://doi.acm.org/10.1145/1541880.1541882

8. Do, T.M.T., Dousse, O., Miettinen, M., Gatica-Perez, D.: A probabilistic kernel method for human mobility prediction with smartphones. Pervasive Mob. Comput. **20**, 13–28 (2015)

9. Farrahi, K., Gatica-Perez, D.: What did you do today? Discovering daily routines from large-scale mobile data. In: Proceedings of the 16th ACM International Conference on Multimedia, pp. 849–852. ACM (2008)

10. Fleury, A., Noury, N., Vacher, M.: Improving supervised classification of activities of daily living using prior knowledge. In: Digital Advances in Medicine, E-Health, and Communication Technologies, p. 131 (2013)

11. Forkan, A.R.M., Khalil, I., Tari, Z., Foufou, S., Bouras, A.: A context-aware approach for long-term behavioural change detection and abnormality prediction in ambient assisted living. Pattern Recogn. **48**(3), 628–641 (2015). http://www.sciencedirect.com/science/article/pii/S0031320314002660

12. Foroughi, H., Aski, B.S., Pourreza, H.: Intelligent video surveillance for monitoring fall detection of elderly in home environments. In: 11th International Conference on Computer and Information Technology, ICCIT 2008, pp. 219–224. IEEE (2008)

13. Franco, C., Demongeot, J., Villemazet, C., Vuillerme, N.: Behavioral telemonitoring of the elderly at home: detection of nycthemeral rhythms drifts from location data. In: 2010 IEEE 24th International Conference on Advanced Information Networking and Applications Workshops (WAINA), pp. 759–766. IEEE (2010)

14. Golder, S.A., Macy, M.W.: Diurnal and seasonal mood vary with work, sleep, and daylength across diverse cultures. Science **333**(6051), 1878–1881 (2011)

15. Hong, X., Nugent, C.D.: Segmenting sensor data for activity monitoring in smart environments. Pers. Ubiquit. Comput. **17**(3), 545–559 (2013)

16. Hsu, H.H., Chen, C.C.: RFID-based human behavior modeling and anomaly detection for elderly care. Mobile Inf. Syst. **6**(4), 341–354 (2010)

17. Jakkula, V.R., Cook, D.J.: Detecting anomalous sensor events in smart home data for enhancing the living experience. Artif. Intell. Smarter Living **11**(201), 1 (2011)

18. Jakkula, V.R., Crandall, A.S., Cook, D.J.: Enhancing anomaly detection using temporal pattern discovery. In: Kameas, A.D., Callagan, V., Hagras, H., Weber, M., Minker, W. (eds.) Advanced Intelligent Environments, pp. 175–194. Springer, US (2009)

19. Kim, S.H., Chung, K.: Emergency situation monitoring service using context motion tracking of chronic disease patients. Clust. Comput. **18**(2), 747–759 (2015). http://dx.doi.org/10.1007/s10586-015-0440-1

20. Kornowski, R., Zeeli, D., Averbuch, M., Finkelstein, A., Schwartz, D., Moshkovitz, M., Weinreb, B., Hershkovitz, R., Eyal, D., Miller, M., et al.: Intensive home-care surveillance prevents hospitalization and improves morbidity rates among elderly patients with severe congestive heart failure. Am. Heart J. **129**(4), 762–766 (1995)

21. Lotfi, A., Langensiepen, C., Mahmoud, S.M., Akhlaghinia, M.J.: Smart homes for the elderly dementia sufferers: identification and prediction of abnormal behaviour. J. Ambient Intell. Humaniz. Comput. **3**(3), 205–218 (2012)

22. Madan, A., Cebrian, M., Lazer, D., Pentland, A.: Social sensing for epidemiological behavior change. In: Proceedings of the 12th ACM International Conference on Ubiquitous Computing, pp. 291–300. ACM (2010)

23. Nasution, A.H., Emmanuel, S.: Intelligent video surveillance for monitoring elderly in home environments. In: IEEE 9th Workshop on Multimedia Signal Processing, MMSP 2007, pp. 203–206. IEEE (2007)

24. Noury, N., Hadidi, T., Laila, M., Fleury, A., Villemazet, C., Rialle, V., Franco, A.: Level of activity, night and day alternation, and well being measured in a smart hospital suite. In: Proceedings of IEEE-EMBC, vol. 8, pp. 20–24 (2008)

25. Novák, M., Biňas, M., Jakab, F.: Unobtrusive anomaly detection in presence of elderly in a smart-home environment. In: ELEKTRO 2012, pp. 341–344. IEEE (2012)
26. Ordóñez, F.J., Toledo, P., Sanchis, A.: Sensor-based Bayesian detection of anomalous living patterns in a home setting. Pers. Ubiquit. Comput. **19**(2), 259–270 (2015). http://dx.doi.org/10.1007/s00779-014-0820-1
27. Pereira, J.D., da Silva e Silva, F.J., Coutinho, L.R., de TácioPereira Gomes, B., Endler, M.: A movement activity recognition pervasive system for patient monitoring in ambient assisted living. In: Proceedings of the 31st Annual ACM Symposium on Applied Computing, pp. 155–161. ACM (2016)
28. Suryadevara, N.K., Mukhopadhyay, S.C.: Wireless sensor network based home monitoring system for wellness determination of elderly. IEEE Sens. J. **12**(6), 1965–1972 (2012)
29. Urwyler, P., Rampa, L., Stucki, R., Büchler, M., Müri, R., Mosimann, U.P., Nef, T.: Recognition of activities of daily living in healthy subjects using two ad-hoc classifiers. Biomed. Eng. Online **14**(1), 1 (2015)
30. Wiles, J.L., Leibing, A., Guberman, N., Reeve, J., Allen, R.E.S.: The meaning of ageing in place to older people. Gerontol. **52**(3), 357–366 (2012)
31. Yoo, J.H., Ko, J.G., Chung, Y.S., Jung, S.U., Kim, K.H., Moon, K.Y., Chung, K.: Design of embedded multimodal biometric systems. In: Third International IEEE Conference on Signal-Image Technologies and Internet-Based System, SITIS 2007, pp. 1058–1062. IEEE (2007)

Human Behavior Analysis from Smartphone Data Streams

Laleh Jalali[1]([✉]), Hyungik Oh[1], Ramin Moazeni[2], and Ramesh Jain[1]

[1] University of California, Irvine, USA
{lalehj,hyungiko,jain}@ics.uci.edu
[2] Santa Clara University, Santa Clara, USA
rmoazzeni@scu.edu

Abstract. In the past decade multimedia systems have started including diverse modes of data to understand complex situations and build
more sophisticated models. Some increasingly common modes in multimedia are intertwined data streams from sensor modalities such as wear-
able/mobile, environmental, and biosensors. These data streams offer
new information sources to model and predict complex world situations
as well as understanding and modeling humans. This paper makes two
contributions to the modeling and analysis of multimodal data in the
context of user behavior analysis. First, it introduces the use of a concept lattice based data fusion technique for recognizing events. Concept
lattices are very effective when enough labeled data samples are not available for supervised machine learning algorithms, but human knowledge is
available to develop classification approaches for recognition. Life events
encode activities of daily living, and environmental events encode states
and state transitions in environmental variables. Second, it introduces a
framework that detects frequent co-occurrence patterns as sequential and
parallel relations among events from multiple event streams. We show
the applicability of our approach in finding interesting human behavior
patterns by using longitudinal mobile data collected from 23 users over
1–2 months.

1 Introduction

Traditionally the term *media* refers to audio, video, image, and text. With the
proliferation of other data modalities such as wearable motion sensors, micro-
electromechanical systems (MEMS), health sensors and environmental sensors,
these data streams are not an exception anymore but an expected media content
in different applications. In various disciplines, information about an underlying
phenomenon might be acquired from different types of sensors. Rarely a single
modality can provide complete knowledge of the phenomenon of interest due
to rich characteristics and complexity of that phenomenon. In order to extract
insight from this data two major challenges arise: (1) How to fuse these modalities into a human understandable abstraction signals that not only preserve the
semantics of the underlying system but also facilitate data analysis? (2) How to

© Springer International Publishing AG 2016
M. Chetouani et al. (Eds.): HBU 2016, LNCS 9997, pp. 68–85, 2016.
DOI: 10.1007/978-3-319-46843-3_5

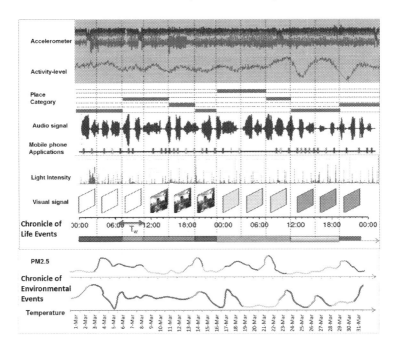

Fig. 1. Chronicle of life events are derived from heterogeneous multimedia content. Chronicle of environmental events are shown as segmented time series data. Each colored segment corresponds to a specific event. (Color figure online)

build conceptual models in an abstraction process for the purpose of *understanding* and *explaining* the underlying system? Detecting events from video streams, audio streams, and text has received considerable interest in multimedia literature. The primary motivation for the event detection in multimedia is that events facilitate indexing and summarizing multimedia data. Westermann and Jain [11,33] show that events in multimedia systems, model real world events as captured by various relevant intertwined and correlated data sources. Thus, events provide an excellent abstraction framework to represent happenings in real world using multimodal heterogeneous data in a human-centric manner, and such multimodal data understanding is an important prerequisite for building meaningful models.

Figure 1 shows two broad categories of data streams. The first category includes sensors that collect heterogeneous personal data from different sources such as an accelerometer and GPS. These data streams are temporally aligned and divided into equal time windows T_w. Within each time window, one or multiple probable life events might be recognized. Life events signifies all daily living activities which are part of daily life. Large amount of data collected from individuals are unlabeled. This means there is no description of the meaning of data or what inference can be drawn. So Unsupervised learning is the next big frontier for finding useful inferences in such data. In this work we propose the use of Formal Concept Analysis (FCA) for data fusion and life event recognition. Concept lattices are very effective when enough labeled data samples are not available for supervised machine learning algorithms, but human knowledge is available to develop classification approaches for recognition.

The second category contains environmental sensory information such as pollution and temperature. These time-series data can be converted to time series of discrete labels through discretization, and meaningful events can be defined on top of these data streams (e.g. a pollution increases suddenly). As data is collected through time, recognized events create a chronicle. A chronicle is a sequence of historical events that covers the entire recording of personal, organizational, social, or environmental events. Event chronicle introduces a new structure over time dimension, and data analysis can be performed at this abstracted level rather than on low-level time series data. These events are not merely a symbol or tag, but a composite datum with multiple facets. According to [27] events can be characterized by six different aspects: time, space, participation/information, relations among events, documentation, and interpretation. For instance:

```
LifeEvent.type=Meeting,
Meeting.Participant="John"
Meeting.Location="DBH Building"
EnvironmentalEvent.type=PM2.5_Increasing
```

After fusing multimodal sensor observations into a human understandable set of events, the next step is analyzing these events to understand co-occurrence relation between them. In this work we aim to infer higher level *behavior patterns* from chronicle of life events, where life events are recognized from longitudinal log data collected by smartphones. We use pattern mining algorithms proposed by Jalali et al. [16] to discover frequent event co-occurrence patterns as sequential and parallel relations among events. This indicates which life events or environmental events frequently occur together. For example:

```
(1) Driving is FOLLOWED BY Meeting WITHIN 1 hour
(2) Browsing-Web happens WHILE Attending-Class
(3) Low-ActivityLevel happens WHILE High-Temperature
```

Our long term vision is to use environmental variables and longitudinal user data to infer diverse frequent patterns that capture different aspects of the user's behavior.

This paper makes two contributions to the modeling and analysis of multimedia data in the context of behavioral trend analysis. First, it introduces a human-centric data fusion technique using events. Life events encode activities of daily living, and environmental events encode states and state transitions in environmental variables. Second, this paper introduces a framework that builds effective user models by harvesting significant patterns as sequential and parallel relations among events. This framework is able to automatically model multimedia information at a high level of abstraction and extract insight from a pool of heterogeneous data. The applicability of this interactive and visual model-building platform is evaluated in finding interesting behavioral patterns of 23 subjects, who carry our Android lifelog app for the duration of 1–2 months. By applying Formal Concept Analysis (FCA) technique, 21 life events are recognized from logged data as discussed in Sect. 3. Section 4 explains event co-occurrence concept for detecting interesting patterns and it follows by the experiments and results in Sect. 5.

2   Related Work

As the number and ubiquity of sensors have grown phenomenally in recent years, human activity recognition using wearable sensors and mobile phones have attracted much attention. There is a rich body of research on activity recognition using Micro-Electro-Mechanical Systems (MEMS) sensors [4]. Lately some multisensor approaches for smartphone-based activity recognition have been developed. A comprehensive survey about activity recognition using mobile phones can be found in [15]. However, these techniques mostly capture low-level physical motion of a user. There is a significant amount of work that uses location sensors to extract high-level information about a person's activities. Routinely visited locations such as home, work, or school can indicate pursued activities such as leisure, working, or picking up someone [19]. However, they do not combine location information with other sensor data from smartphones to detect high-level life events. In another interesting application, Bao et al. [5] explored user status and transition as an intrinsic string that connects daily user activities. In their work, user status was estimated from mobility trajectories, app usage and to communication patterns. In an effort to tap the full potential of smartphones in context-aware application, A.K. Dey et al. introduce a conceptual context toolkit called *CORTEXT* [8]. They present a mobile data-logging toolkit, AWARE [9], which provides capturing, inferring, and generating context on mobile devices. *CORTEXT* allows researchers to define rules, contexts, and services by integrating sentient objects and an event-based communication protocol [6,9]. Another context-aware application is presented by H. Oh et al. [22]. They capture real-time situations of a user by tracking and analyzing transitions of collected contexts from different smartphone sensors. finding the best recognizable and available notification moments is one of the applications of their system. What makes our life event recognition component different from the above mentioned works, is utilizing FCA as a means to fuse heterogeneous and noisy context data from smartphone sensors to recognize life events from unlabeled data collected from real-life environment.

With the trend of activity recognition, Alan F. Smeaton et al. emphasize the importance of lifelogging as *a phenomenon whereby people can digitally record their own daily lives in varying amounts of detail, for a variety of purposes* [12]. They consider the application of lifelogging in different domains including medical (i.e. memory support), behavioral science (i.e. analysis of quality of life), work-related (i.e. auto-recording of tasks), etc. [26]. They suggest an end to end lifelogging solution with cutting edge components (i.e. gathering, enriching, segmenting, keyframe, annotation and narrative) for extracting meaningful knowledge from one's lifelog data. Along the same direction, Qiu et al. use a smartphone to gather and organize e-memory, to digitally encode all life experiences [25] The importance of lifelogging give raise to quantified self movement [12], which tracks, collects, and extracts knowledge using sensor devices for better understanding human behaviors. In another setting, for providing better privacy guarantee to users, MobileMiner [28], introduces a middleware to extract user behavior patterns from mobile data and perform pattern mining on the phone itself.

Understanding temporal relations enables us to learn from the past and build models to predict and plan for the future. There are several visualization tools for time-oriented data in the literature. A complete survey of them can be found in [2]. These tools are merely visual representation of multivariate time-series data. Events, on the other hand, can be used for trend analysis and pattern recognition, which in fact lifts the analysis to yet a higher level of abstraction. Tominski [29] focuses on visualizing user defined events to bring the needs of users into focus. Some applications such as TimeSearcher [13], DataJewel [3], and LifeLines [24] offer visualizations that cluster results and highlight temporal patterns. We emphasize that none of the systems discussed above enables event recognition in the process of multimodal data fusion and visualizations of patterns as relations between these events.

Sensor-based approaches are extensively adopted in human behavior modeling and health behavior promotion. [17] utilized an android app to promote regular physical activity in users with sedentary life style. In a different setting, [32] looks for correlations between academic performance and the averages of the low level sensor data (i.e., activity and mobility) for college students. Wang et al. [31] try to find a correlation between students' stress and their activity level, sleep, and academic performance. Although using mobile phone for such studies is encouraging, we believe that utilization of multimodal sensors for behavior analysis has developed to a point where it is appropriate to begin emphasizing on more advanced data processing techniques that result in meaningful models rather than relying heavily on correlational statistics.

3   Events: Human-Centric Data Fusion Approach

Most machine algorithms decompose multimedia content to data segments such as shots, scenes, etc., and index them using low-level feature vectors or limited higher-level metadata (e.g. visual concepts), while humans remember real life using past experience structured in the form of events. So events are the basic components of how humans perceive the world, and memories are shaped through associations between the perceived events. The necessity of formal event models for the description of real life events has been acknowledged, and a number of such models have been developed [1, 27].

3.1   Importance of Life Events

The inputs to hearing, vision, and the other senses are continuous, dynamic, and comprise huge amounts of data each second. However, human conscious experience seems to resolve into a manageable number of more-or-less discrete entities, most prominently *objects* and *events*. The term **event perception** encompasses a range of cognitive techniques involving the processing of temporally extended dynamic information. In this process, our brain picks up intervals of time and distinguishes them from other intervals to form meaningful events. Moreover, Our brain tends to automatically seek patterns (relations among events) [14]. With this capability, our brain consolidates multiple events and their relations as a piece of *memory* or *knowledge* (2(a)).

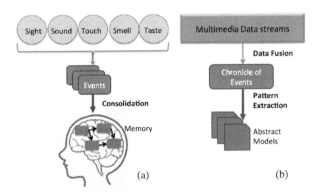

Fig. 2. Event perception and memory recall in humans resemble multimedia data fusion and model building.

Cognitive researchers are focused on the formation of what are known as *memory assemblies* [34]. These are networks of neurons, connected via synapses, which can store a particular segment of a memory as an event. When a memory is being recalled, its particular assemblies piece related events together to produce a whole. As shown in Fig. 2(b), our methodology for processing multimedia data and building models of the underlying system is in fact inspired by a human's capability in analyzing multimodal data and constructing abstract models of the real world.

3.2   Life Log

Table 1 shows life log attributes collected from a smartphone. Location data has venue_name and venue_type attributes for a specific latitude and longitude coordinate (e.g. name: Panini, type: restaurant). Venue type information is obtained from Google place API by using latitude and longitude data of Google-play-service API. Media is a Boolean attribute that monitors whether the user listens to music or watches video. Transition is a Boolean attribute that determines whether user's location has changed from a certain venue type to another

Table 1. Data streams from smartphone and list of derived attributes from each stream

Data Stream	Attribute
time	time_window, unix_timestamp, weekday/weekend
activity	activity_type (standing still, tilting, walking, running, bicycling, and in vehicle), activity_level $\in[0,4]$
location	latitude, longitude venue_name, venue_type
step	step_count
application	app_name
photo	photo_count
light	light_value $\in[0,1000]$
phone status	screen_on, screen_off
media	play_time
sound	sound_setting $\subset\{$(silence, vibration, or bell)$\}$
call	call_type $\subset\{$(missed, rejected, incoming or outgoing)$\}$
transition	changes in venue type

Table 2. Selected list of life event. Category (a) shows life events derived from sensor fusion and category (b) shows life events results from raw context data from smartphone.

Category	Method	Life event
(a)	Context Fusion with FCA	Studying, Sleeping, Vehicle Transportation, Dining, Attending Class, Walking, Running, Cycling, Exercise, Leaving Home, Arriving Home
(b)	Raw Context	Interacting with Phone, Surfing Web, Social Networking, Checking Email, Sending SMS, Phone Call, Watching Video, Skype Call

between two contiguous 5-min intervals. These attributes are collected for each 5-minute interval. Interval segments are then fed to life event recognition module.

Table 2 shows a selected group of life event and their corresponding recognition method. The life event recognition module can either recognize one of the events in the first category using FCA as a *context fusion* technique, or return an *unknown* event. Contextual information related to application usage on a smartphone can be utilized to determine one of the events in the second category of life events. We assume that life events in the first category are mutually exclusive in a sense that two (or more) of them can not happen simultaneously in a 5-minute interval. However, they can happen in parallel with life events in the second category, e.g. a user might check her email while attending class.

3.3 Life Event Recognition

Recognizing life events from human physical activity and surrounding contexts is a challenging problem. Learning-based approaches are good at recognizing low-level physical activities (e.g. walking, jogging, etc.) from a limited number of wearable sensors [4]. However, it is difficult to incorporate domain knowledge in their learning process and extract more high-level semantics related to life events. Moreover, collected observational data is noisy and there is not enough **labeled** data available for training purposes since labeling human activities are very tedious. Thus, Formal Concept Analysis (FCA) can be utilized to resolve some of these issues.

Definitions. The theoretical foundation of concept lattice relies on the mathematical lattice theory [7]. Concept lattice is used to represent the order relation of concepts.

Definition 1: A context is defined by a triple (G, M, R), where G and M are two sets, and R is a relation between them. The elements of G are called objects, while the elements of M are called attributes.

For example, Fig. 3(a) represents a context in form of a cross table. $G(o_1, o_2, o_3, o_4, o_5, o_6, o_7)$ is the object set and $M(a_1, a_2, a_3, a_4, a_5, a_6, a_7, a_8, a_9)$ is the attribute set. The crosses in the table describe the relation R between G and M, which means an object verifies an attribute.

Definition 2: Given a subset $A \subseteq G$ of objects from a context (G, M, R), we define an operator that produces the set A' of their common attributes for $A \subseteq G$ to know which attributes from M are common to all these objects:

$$A' = \{m \in M \quad | \quad gRm \forall g \in A\}$$

Dually, we define $\acute{B}$ for subset of attributes $B \subseteq M$, B' denotes the set consisting of those objects in G that have all the attributes from B:

$$B' = \{g \in G \quad | \quad gRm \forall m \in B\}$$

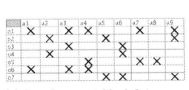

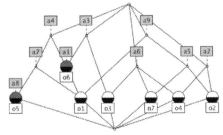

(a) Sample cross table defining relation between a set of objects and attributes.

(b) Concept lattice derived from cross table by applying NextClosure algorithm.

Fig. 3. An example of context (G, M, R) and its equivalent concept lattice.

These two operators are called the Galois connection of (G, M, R). These operators are used to determine a formal concept.

Definition 3: A formal concept of the context (G, M, R) is a pair (A, B) with $A \subseteq G$, $B \subseteq M$, $A = B'$, and $B = A'$. A is called extent and B is called intent. So if B is an attribute set, B' is an object set, and then $(B')'$ is an attribute set. So the following axioms hold:

$$B \subseteq M \Rightarrow B'' \subseteq M$$
$$A \subseteq G \Rightarrow A'' \subseteq G$$

Definition 4: If (A_1, B_1) and (A_2, B_2) are concepts, $A_1 \subseteq A_2$ (or $B_2 \subseteq B_1$), then we say that there is a hierarchical order between (A_1, B_1) and (A_2, B_2). All concepts with the hierarchical order of concepts form a complete lattice called concept lattice.

To map the above definitions to life event recognition problem, we consider life events as objects, and sensor measurements as attributes. The lattice algorithm to build formal concepts and concept lattice plays an essential role in the application of concept lattice. Many algorithms for generating concept lattices are published such as Ganter (NextClosure) [10], Gerhand [23], Norris [21], and Valtchev [30]. Kuznetsov et al. [18] performed a performance analysis of these algorithms and gave preference to Ganter's algorithm with respect to time complexity.

Lattice Construction Algorithm. NextClosure algorithm by Ganter [10] is one of the most well known algorithms in FCA. Figure 3(b) shows a lattice constructed from the cross table using this algorithm. The principle of NextClosure algorithm uses the characteristic vector which represents arbitrary subsets A of M, to enumerate all concepts of (G, M, R). Given $A \subseteq M$, $M = \{a_1, a_2, \dots, a_m\}$, $A \rightarrow A''$ is the closure operator. The NextClosure algorithm proves that if we know an arbitrary attribute subset A, the next concept (the smallest one of all concepts that is larger than A) with respect to the lexicographical order is $A \oplus a_i$, where $\oplus$ is defined by:

$$A \oplus a_i = (A \cap (a_1, \dots, a_{i-1}) \cup a_i)''$$

where $A \subseteq M$ and $a_i \in M$, a_i being the largest element of M with $A < A \oplus a_i$ by lexicographical order. In other words, for $a_i \in M \backslash A$, from the largest element to smaller one of $M \backslash A$, we calculate $A \oplus a_i$, until we find the first time $A < A \oplus a_i$, then $A \oplus a_i$ is the next concept.

We apply NextClosure algorithm to build a comprehensive lattice from our pre-defined cross table (as shown in Table 3) that capture the relation between life events and their common attributes. Considering $|L| =$ number of life events, and $|A| =$ number of attributes, the time complexity of building the lattice is $O(|L|^2 \times |A|)$. The constructed lattice is visually depicted in Fig. 4.

Table 3. Cross table of generalized relationship between life events and their attributes

Life Event \ Attr	Time								Activity											Location															Sensor			Fun										Setting		Other	
	time_band						week		physical_activity						activity_level					venue_type															light			media		app_usage				photo_taken				sound		Call	
	T/B_0	T/B_1	T/B_2	T/B_3	T/B_4	T/B_5	W_0	W_1	P.A_0	P.A_1	P.A_2	P.A_3	P.A_4	P.A_5	A.L_0	A.L_1	A.L_2	A.L_3	A.L_4	home	school	university	acm.buildin	entertainm	gym	nightlife spl	outdoors	store	mall	shop	food	cafe	restaurant	residential	E.L_0	E.L_1	E.L_2	M_0	M_1	A.U_0	A.U_1	A.U_2	A.U_3	T/P_0	T/P_1	T/P_2	T/P_3	S_0	S_1	C.L_0	C.L_1
Sleeping	X	X	X				X	X	X						X					X															X	X												X			X
Studying				X	X		X	X		X	X						X	X		X	X	X													X	X				X	X	X	X		X	X	X	X	X	X		X
Vehicle Commute	X	X	X	X	X	X	X	X		X	X						X	X				X													X	X	X	X	X	X	X	X	X	X	X	X	X	X	X	X		X
Dining		X	X	X	X		X	X		X	X						X	X											X		X		X	X	X	X	X	X	X	X	X	X	X	X	X	X	X	X	X	X	X		X
Attending Class	X	X	X				X			X	X						X	X		X	X	X	X												X														X			X
Walking	X	X	X	X	X	X	X	X			X	X					X	X				X	X	X	X	X	X								X	X	X	X	X	X	X	X	X						X	X		X
Running	X	X	X	X	X	X	X	X	X			X					X	X		X		X													X	X	X			X	X							X			X
Cycling	X	X	X	X	X	X	X	X					X				X	X		X		X													X	X	X			X	X							X	X		X
Exercising		X	X	X			X	X						X				X		X		X													X	X													X			X

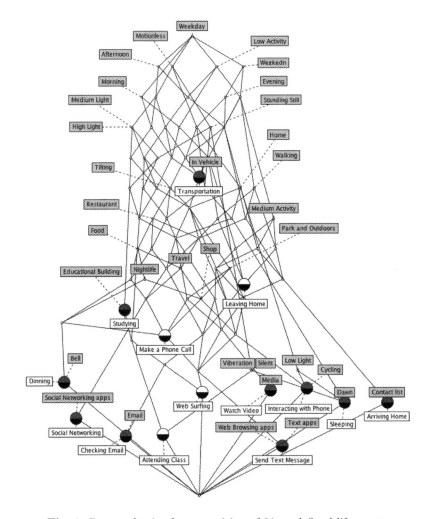

Fig. 4. Concept lattice for recognition of 21 predefined life events.

Lattice Navigation Algorithm. Once the lattice is constructed from a pre-defined set of concepts, the next step is to recognize life events using such constructed lattice from observational sensor data. We use backtracking depth first search algorithm for this purpose. To identify a life event, the system collects all the perceptible context information and feed them to the lattice. If the context satisfies the conditions of a life event, then it is identified. For example, an incoming life-log information, $S_{lifelog} = \{$00:00 - 03:59, week, standing_still, sedentary, home, environmental_light_low, media_false, app_no_use, photo_no_use, sound bell, call_no_calling$\}$, will navigate the concept lattice by following the backtracking algorithm and *sleeping* event will be predicted.

4   Co-occurrence Pattern Mining

Mining frequent patterns is an important area of data mining where one discovers sub-structures that occur often in structured data. However, when dealing with heterogeneous unstructured or semi-structured multimodal data, detecting frequent patterns is a challenging task. In this paper we use the concepts of *conditional sequential* and *concurrent* patterns and pattern mining algorithm from event streams as introduced in [16]. Conditional sequence operator $(\rho_1; \omega_{\Delta t_1} \ \rho_2)$ detects if pattern expression ρ_1 is followed by pattern expression ρ_2 *within* Δt time units. Δt is called the time lag or temporal restriction between two successive patterns. Also concurrency operator $(\rho_1 \parallel \rho_2)$ detects if patterns occur in parallel. Unlike sequence, any order is allowed, and there has to be a non-empty overlap interval among the patterns. In their work, co-occurrence concept only applied to an ordered sequence of events. For example if E_j usually occurs after E_i (within a specific time), these two events are considered to be co-occurring. However, co-occurrence concept is broader and can happen between events without any specific order or time lag as long as those events are temporally overlapped. We use the keyword *FOLLOWED BY* for the former, and *WHILE* for the latter. Hence we introduce new definition of event co-occurrence as follows:

Sequential Co-occurrence: For a pair of events E_i and E_j, co-occurrence with temporal offset Δt is the frequency count of E_j following E_i within Δt time lag.

$$Seq - CO_{E_i,E_j}[\Delta t] = \frac{Count(E_i; \omega_{\Delta t} E_j)}{Count(E_i)} \tag{1}$$

Concurrent Co-occurrence: For a pair of events E_i and E_j, co-occurrence is the frequency count of E_i and E_j occurring with no particular order while $[E_i.t_s, E_i.t_e] \bigcap [E_j.t_s, E_j.t_e] \neq \emptyset$.

$$Con - CO_{E_i,E_j} = \frac{Count(E_i \parallel E_j)}{\frac{1}{2}(Count(E_i) + Count(E_j))} \tag{2}$$

Effective models can be built by finding significant and interesting co-occurrence relationships between events. In most pattern mining techniques, occurrence frequency is the main criteria to assess the significance of a pattern. However, using high frequency thresholds may reveal only the common knowledge while low thresholds result in an explosion of discovered patterns. To solve this problem we apply a visual analysis technique using co-occurrence matrices and engage a human in the model building process where an analyst can visually extract interesting patterns. As shown in Fig. 6, x and y axes of the matrix are composed of event types in a specific application domain. Sequential Co-occurrence generates a matrix for any given Δt. Each cell of the matrix is the co-occurrence value calculated from Eqs. 1 or 2 for a given pair of events.

5   Evaluation and Results

In previous sections we explained how multiple sources of information (e.g. location, motion, etc.) can be semantically fused to recognize activities of a person in the form of life events and how effective models can be built by finding significant sequential or concurrent co-occurrence patterns. In this section we evaluate the applicability of our framework in understanding the behavior of individuals using smartphones as the main source of personal information. The technological and social characteristics of smartphone make it a useful tool in behavioral analysis. The device is willingly carried by a large fraction of people and allows unobtrusive and cost-effective access to previously inaccessible sources of data on everyday activity patterns. Also the changes of these patterns through time and the effect of environmental conditions on such patterns can be investigated.

5.1   Data Collection

We developed an Android-based lifelog app that collected data continuously without user intervention. Table 1 demonstrates the type of sensors utilized in this study and the information derived from them. All participants in the study were voluntarily recruited from a mobile Programming class, a computer science programming class offered to both undergraduate and graduate students during spring quarter in 2014. 65 students enrolled in the class and 31 joined the study. As the quarter progressed, 8 users dropped out of the study. From 23 remaining users, 12 were undergraduate and 11 were graduate students. Users used their own Android devices to run our lifelog app and carried the phones with them throughout the day. Data was collected without any user interaction and uploaded to the cloud daily. The data collection phase lasted for 4 weeks for the class. However, 4 users continued to collect data for another 4 weeks.

GPS tracking generates large sets of geographic data, and needs to be transformed to be useful for life event recognition and behavior analysis. We are interested in the type of a location/venue that a user visits rather than its coordinates. The reverse geo-coding is done by using Google place API. In other words, our behavior analysis system distinguishes between locations only if it helps determine what the user is doing. The venue categories we incorporated in this study are: *arts and entertainment, collage and university, academic building,*

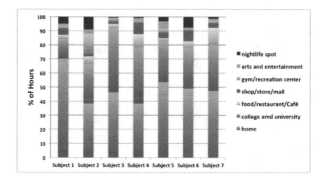

Fig. 5. Percentage of hours multiple subjects spent at different locations.

gym, nightlife spot, outdoors and recreation, store, mall, shop, food, cafe, restaurant. Also we asked users for their *home* location once the app was launched. Figure 5 shows location distribution for 7 users based on the percentage of time they spend at each location. The amount of time spent at different places reveals a lot of information about a user. For instance Fig. 5 suggests that user 1 spent the majority of her time at home while user 3 spent considerable time at school. Also user 2 visits the gym frequently while food places and malls are of interest for users 7 and 4 respectively.

5.2   Sequential Co-Occurrence: Commute Behavior and Activity Trends

The objective of this experiment is to find patterns of commute behavior from life event stream. By generating sequential co-occurrence matrices with different temporal offsets, co-occurrences between *leaving home* and *arriving home* and commute types such as *walking, transportation,* and *cycling* is studied. Figure 6 demonstrates the results for 3 different subjects. Figure 6(a) indicates commute pattern: *Leaving Home [0–15 min] Transportation* with co-occurrence value of 0.87, which means with 87 % probability the subject used a vehicle within 15 min after leaving home. By increasing the temporal offset to 1 h, the probability reaches 98 %. Leaving home followed by cycling and cycling followed by attending class is a commute pattern observable for another subject in Fig. 6(b,c). Finally, Fig. 6(d) shows walking commute pattern to/from school for the third subject.

Since the study was conducted for four weeks, we could analyze the change of commute behavior and activity level in some participants. Figures 7 and 8 show sequential occurrence frequency of multiple patterns for two different subjects. The occurrence frequency of a pattern gets accumulated through time. So a sharp slope within an interval in the graph indicates the pattern was repeated often during that time, while a flat line suggests the pattern did not occur. Figure 7 implies that for one participant, activity level trend and vehicle transportation did not show any changes between subsequent weeks. However, a clear decrease

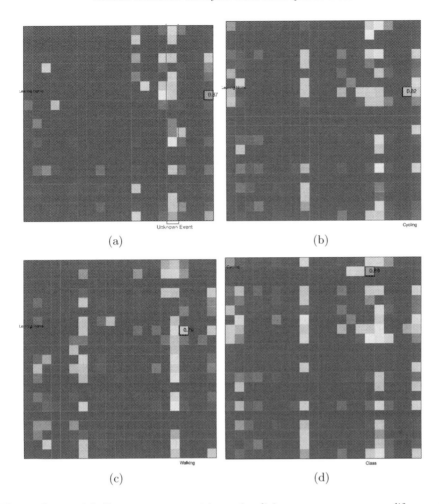

(a)

(b)

(c)

(d)

Fig. 6. Sequential Co-occurrence matrices visualizing co-occurrence on life event streams. (a) Co-ocurrence between leaving home followed by using car within 15 min = 0.87. (b) Co-ocurrence between leaving home and cycling within 30 min = 0.82. (c) Co-ocurrence between leaving home and walking within 15 min = 0.79. (d) Co-ocurrence between cycling and attending class within 1 h = 0.89.

in using bicycle for commute purposes is visible in Fig. 8 during the third and forth weeks, which in fact corresponds to a decrease in activity level.

5.3   Concurrent Co-occurrence: Multitasking Behavior

As mentioned in Sect. 3, concurrent co-occurrence examines the co-occurrence relation between events that might be temporally overlapped. Some of the life events explained in Sect. 2 might happen in parallel. For instance, dining might be concurrent with sending text or making a phone call. In this experiment we

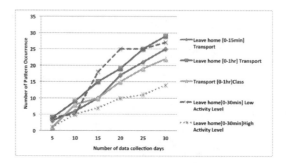

Fig. 7. Transportation and activity-level patterns. No major change is observed in commute behavior

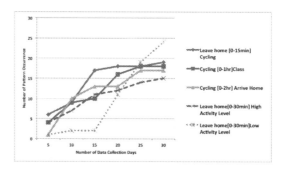

Fig. 8. Transportation and activity-level patterns. Commute behavior has changed during the second half of study.

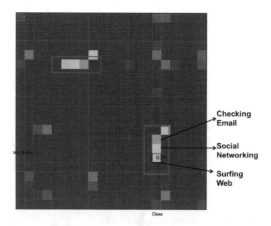

Fig. 9. Concurrent Co-occurrence matrix visualizing co-occurrence on life event streams.

used concurrent co-occurrence matrix to investigate users' interaction with the phone **while** they engage in other activities. Figure 9 displays an interesting result for one of the subjects. As shown, there is a clear co-occurrence between surfing the web, checking email, and using social networking apps while the person was attending a class. This analysis reflects multitasking in classroom and indicates that the students were bored or distracted during classes.

5.4   The Effect of Environmental Factors on Behavior

It's now apparent that exposure to some air pollutant (Particulate Matter PM2.5) has consequences for human health and life expectancy. Exposure to fine particulate matter is particularly dangerous since these small particles penetrate deep into the lungs and may also affect other aspects of human life. This experiment is devoted to examine the associations between certain environmental conditions and human behavior. The main question is whether short term exposure to PM2.5 or certain climate change conditions has any bearing on an individual's physical activity, and whether it causes any deviation in routine activities. By GPS tracking, the closest pollution and weather stations to user's current location is found, and ambient temperature and PM2.5 data is collected. Unified event streams are then constructed by abstracting trends of time-series data using Symbolic Aggregate approXimation (SAX) algorithm [20] with alphabet size 3 (a,b,c symbols). For each data stream, 7 event types (ab/bc = increase, ac = suddenly increase, ca = suddenly decrease, cb/ba = decrease, aaa = stay low, bbb = medium, ccc = stay high) are defined as color coded in Fig. 1. After processing sequential co-occurrences and concurrent co-occurrences between life event stream and PM2.5/temperature event stream we found a few occurrences of the following patterns for multiple subjects:

```
-> AcrivityLevel_Low WHILE temperature_Increasing
-> PM2.5_SuddenlyIncreases FOLLOWED BY transportation WITHIN 3 hours
-> Walking WHILE PM2.5_StayLow
```

Although the above patterns might be an indication of how users commute or how active they are in different environmental situations, a longitudinal study with longer duration shall be performed to assess more reliable patterns.

6   Conclusion and Future Work

In this paper, we presented a framework to discover new knowledge from rich multimodal data and build effective models in the context of behavioral trend analysis. First we introduced a human-centric data fusion technique using events. Life events encode activities of daily living and environmental events encode external situations. Second, we introduced the co-occurrence concept within a visual interactive framework that facilitates significant pattern extraction and model building. A demo of the system is provided in a YouTube channel[1].

---

[1] https://youtu.be/mmu9EFYFPjE.

In the future we will extend the list of life events by adding other sources of information such as user's calendar and social network activities. Also, we will improve our lifelog app to get feedback from user regarding the detected events. Hence, not only we will access labeled activity data from user's explicit input, but also we will be able to improve and revise the relation between events and their corresponding attributes in the concept lattice.

References

1. A data model and format for collecting and distributing eventinformation. https://iptc.org/standards/eventsml-g2/
2. Aigner, W., Miksch, S., Müller, W., Schumann, H., Tominski, C.: Visualizing time-oriented data - a systematic view. Comput. Graph. **31**(3), 401–409 (2007)
3. Ankerst, M., Jones, D.H., Kao, A., Wang, C.: Datajewel: tightly integrating visualization with temporal data mining. In: VDM@ ICDM, p. 113 (2003)
4. Bao, L., Intille, S.S.: Activity recognition from user-annotated acceleration data. In: Ferscha, A., Mattern, F. (eds.) Pervasive 2004. LNCS, vol. 3001, pp. 1–17. Springer, Heidelberg (2004). doi:10.1007/978-3-540-24646-6_1
5. Bao, X., Gong, N.Z., Hu, B., Shen, Y., Jin, H.: Connect the dots by understanding user status and transitions. In: Proceedings of the 2014 ACM International Joint Conference on Pervasive and Ubiquitous Computing: Adjunct Publication, pp. 361–366. ACM (2014)
6. Biegel, G., Cahill, V.,: A framework for developing mobile, context-aware applications. In: Proceedings of the Second IEEE Annual Conference on Pervasive Computing and Communications, PerCom 2004, pp. 361–365. IEEE (2004)
7. Birkhoff, G., Birkhoff, G., Birkhoff, G., Birkhoff, G.: Lattice Theory, vol. 25. American Mathematical Society, New York (1948)
8. Dey, A.K., Abowd, G.D., Salber, D.: A conceptual framework and a toolkit for supporting the rapid prototyping of context-aware applications. Hum. Comput. Interact. **16**(2), 97–166 (2001)
9. Ferreira, D., Kostakos, V., Dey, A.K.: AWARE: mobile context instrumentation framework. Front. ICT **2**(6), 1–9 (2015)
10. Ganter, B.: Two Basic Algorithms in Concept Analysis. Springer, New York (2010)
11. Gupta, A., Jain, R.: Managing event information: modeling, retrieval, and applications. Synth. Lect. Data Manag. **3**(4), 1–141 (2011)
12. Gurrin, C., Smeaton, A.F., Doherty, A.R.: Lifelogging: personal big data. Found. Trends Inf. Retrieval **8**(1), 1–125 (2014)
13. Hochheiser, H., Shneiderman, B.: Interactive exploration of time series data. In: Jantke, K.P., Shinohara, A. (eds.) DS 2001. LNCS (LNAI), vol. 2226, pp. 441–446. Springer, Heidelberg (2001). doi:10.1007/3-540-45650-3_38
14. Hudson, V.M., Schrodt, P.A., Whitmer, R.D.: A new kind of social science? Moving ahead with reverse wolfram models applied to event data. In: International Studies Association, Honolulu (2005)
15. Incel, O.D., Kose, M., Ersoy, C.: A review and taxonomy of activity recognition on mobile phones. BioNanoScience **3**(2), 145–171 (2013)
16. Jalali, L., Jain, R.: Bringing deep causality to multimedia data streams. In Proceedings of the 23rd Annual ACM Conference on Multimedia Conference, pp. 221–230. ACM (2015)

17. King, A.C., Hekler, E.B., Grieco, L.A., Winter, S.J., Sheats, J.L., Buman, M.P., Banerjee, B., Robinson, T.N., Cirimele, J.: Harnessing different motivational frames via mobile phones to promote daily physical activity and reduce sedentary behavior in aging adults. PloS one **8**(4), e62613 (2013)
18. Kuznetsov, S.O., Obiedkov, S.A.: Comparing performance of algorithms for generating concept lattices. J. Exper. Theoret. Artif. Intell. **14**(2–3), 189–216 (2002)
19. Liao, L., Fox, D., Kautz, H.: Extracting places and activities from GPS traces using hierarchical conditional random fields. Int. J. Robot. Res. **26**(1), 119–134 (2007)
20. Lin, J., Keogh, E., Wei, L., Lonardi, S.: Experiencing SAX: a novel symbolic representation of time series. Data Mining Knowl. Disc. **15**(2), 107–144 (2007)
21. Nourine, L., Raynaud, O.: A fast algorithm for building lattices. Inf. Process. Lett. **71**(5), 199–204 (1999)
22. Oh, H., Jalali, L., Jain, R.: An intelligent notification system using context from real-time personal activity monitoring. In: 2015 IEEE International Conference on Multimedia and Expo (ICME), pp. 1–6. IEEE (2015)
23. Oosthuizen, G.D.: The use of a lattice in knowledge processing (1992)
24. Plaisant, C., Milash, B., Rose, A., Widoff, S., Shneiderman, B.: Lifelines: visualizing personal histories. In: Proceedings of the SIGCHI Conference on Human Factors Incomputing Systems, pp. 221–227. ACM (1996)
25. Qiu, Z., Gurrin, C., Doherty, A.R., Smeaton, A.F.: A Real-Time Life Experience Logging Tool. Springer, New York (2012)
26. Qiu, Z., Gurrin, C., Smeaton, A.F.: Evaluating access mechanisms for multimodal representations of lifelogs. In: Tian, Q., Sebe, N., Qi, G.-J., Huet, B., Hong, R., Liu, X. (eds.) MMM 2016. LNCS, vol. 9516, pp. 574–585. Springer, Heidelberg (2016). doi:10.1007/978-3-319-27671-7_48
27. Scherp, A., Mezaris, V.: Survey on modeling and indexing events in multimedia. Multimedia Tools Appl. **70**(1), 7–23 (2014)
28. Srinivasan, V., Moghaddam, S., Mukherji, A., Rachuri, K.K., Xu, C., Tapia, E.M.: MobileMiner: mining your frequent patterns on your phone. In: Proceedings of the 2014 ACM International Joint Conference on Pervasive and Ubiquitous Computing, pp. 389–400. ACM (2014)
29. Tominski, C.: Event based visualization for user centered visual analysis. Ph.D. thesis, University of Rostock (2006)
30. Valtchev, P., Missaoui, R., Lebrun, P.: A partition-based approach towards constructing Galois (concept) lattices. Discrete Math. **256**(3), 801–829 (2002)
31. Wang, R., Chen, F., Chen, Z., Li, T., Harari, G., Tignor, S., Zhou, X., Ben-Zeev, D., Campbell, A.T.: StudentLife: assessing mental health, academic performance and behavioral trends of college students using smartphones. In: Proceedings of the 2014 ACM International Joint Conference on Pervasive and Ubiquitous Computing, pp. 3–14. ACM (2014)
32. Wang, R., Harari, G., Hao, P., Zhou, X., Campbell, A.T.: SmartGPA: how smartphones can assess and predict academic performance of college students. In: Proceedings of the 2015 ACM International Joint Conference on Pervasive and Ubiquitous Computing, pp. 295–306. ACM (2015)
33. Westermann, U., Jain, R.: E - A generic event model for event-centric multimedia data management in eChronicle applications. In: Proceedings of the 22nd International Conference on Data Engineering Workshops. IEEE (2006)
34. Zenke, F., Agnes, E.J., Gerstner, W.: Diverse synaptic plasticity mechanisms orchestrated to form and retrieve memories in spiking neural networks. Nat. Commun. **6** (2015)

Gesture and Movement Analysis

Sign Language Recognition for Assisting the Deaf in Hospitals

Necati Cihan Camgöz[1][(✉)], Ahmet Alp Kındıroğlu[2], and Lale Akarun[2]

[1] University of Surrey, Guildford, Surrey GU2 7XH, UK
n.camgoz@surrey.ac.uk
[2] Department of Computer Engineering, Boğaziçi University, Istanbul, Turkey
{alp.kindiroglu,akarun}@boun.edu.tr

Abstract. In this study, a real-time, computer vision based sign language recognition system aimed at aiding hearing impaired users in a hospital setting has been developed. By directing them through a tree of questions, the system allows the user to state their purpose of visit by answering between four to six questions. The deaf user can use sign language to communicate with the system, which provides a written transcript of the exchange. A database collected from six users was used for the experiments. User independent tests without using the tree-based interaction scheme yield a 96.67 % accuracy among 1257 sign samples belonging to 33 sign classes. The experiments evaluated the effectiveness of the system in terms of feature selection and spatio-temporal modelling. The combination of hand position and movement features modelled by Temporal Templates and classified by Random Decision Forests yielded the best results. The tree-based interaction scheme further increased the recognition performance to more than 97.88 %.

Keywords: Sign language recognition · Assistive computer vision · Human computer interaction

1 Introduction

Sign Languages are the main communication medium of the hearing impaired. They are visual languages in which concepts are conveyed through the positioning, shape and movements of hands, arms and facial expressions. Similar to spoken languages, sign languages developed over time in local communities. For this reason, they show great variation from spoken languages and across other sign languages.

The education of the hearing impaired is a difficult task. Since they are socially isolated due to a communication barrier, they have difficulty learning the spoken language, even in its written form. Therefore literacy of spoken and written language is considerably lower for the hearing impaired. This greatly impedes their integration into society and causes difficulties in receiving education, finding jobs and using everyday public services such as healthcare and banking.

© Springer International Publishing AG 2016
M. Chetouani et al. (Eds.): HBU 2016, LNCS 9997, pp. 89–101, 2016.
DOI: 10.1007/978-3-319-46843-3_6

However, laws mandate the provisioning of assistance to the hearing impaired by providing translators on demand. While it would have increased accessibility greatly, problems were present in its application as there simply were not that many Turkish Sign Language (TİD) translators available. A practical solution was found by making sign language call centers available. However, they had their drawbacks as the call centers had to employ large numbers of translators to service a large deaf population. The ideal solution to this problem is to have software that performs automatic sign language to spoken language translation, thus allowing the hearing impaired people to express themselves in public institutions to receive services.

With the development of machine learning and computer vision algorithms and the availability of different sign language databases, there has been an increasing number of studies in Sign Language Recognition (SLR). Since the work of Starner and Pentland [16] there have been many studies attempting to recognize sign language gestures using spatio-temporal modeling methods such as Hidden Markov Models (HMMs) [14] and Dynamic Time Warping (DTW) [1] based methods. Other approaches, such as Parallel Hidden Markov Models (PaHMMs) [19] and HMM-based threshold model [10], are also used in gesture and sign language recognition systems. Chai et al. [4] used DTW based classifiers to develop a translation system that interprets Chinese Sign Language to Spoken Language and vice versa. In more recent studies, Pitsikalis and Theodorakis et al. [13,18] used DTW to match subunits in Greek Sign Language for recognition purposes.

Prior to the release of consumer depth cameras, such as the Microsoft Kinect sensor [22], many computer vision researchers had to use color and data gloves, embedded accelerometers and video cameras to capture a users hand and body movements for sign language recognition [12]. However, the Microsoft Kinect sensor provides color image, depth map, and real-time human pose information [15], by which it diminishes the dependency to such variety of sensors.

Recently, there has been an increase in studies aimed at developing prototype applications with sign language based user interfaces. One of the earliest applications was the TESSA (Text and Sign Support Assistant) [5], that was developed for the UK Post Offices to assist a post office clerk in communicating with a Deaf person. The TESSA system translates a clerks speech into British Sign Language (BSL) and then displays the signs to the screen with an avatar to a Deaf customer at the post office. The authors used the entropic speech recognizer and performed semantic mapping on a "best match" basis to recognize the most phonetically close phrase. Lopez-Ludena et al. [11] have also designed an automatic translation system for bus information that translates speech to Spanish Sign Language (LSE) and sign language to speech.

In [20], Weaver and Starner introduced SMARTSign, which aims to help the hearing parents of deaf children with learning and practicing ASL via a mobile phone application. The authors share the feedback they received from the parents on the usability and accessibility of the SMARTSign system. In [9], sign language tutoring is performed using a signing robot and interaction tests are used to asses system success. In [21], an avatar based sign language game is developed for teaching first grade curriculum in sign language to primary school children and assessing their knowledge.

When a deaf person arrives at a hospital, if he/she does not know how to read and write in spoken language, it is often a troublesome practice to communicate. To overcome this communication barrier, a sign language recognition platform called HospiSign was created. When deployed on a computer with a Microsoft Kinect v2 sensor, HospiSign works as a reception desk, welcoming deaf users and allowing them to express their purpose of visit.

The user interface of HospiSign was presented in [17]. In this paper, we focus on the sign language recognition aspects of the system. We proposed using several features, temporal modelling techniques and classification methods for sign language recognition. As features, we extracted upper body pose, hand shape, hand position and hand movement features from the data provided by the Microsoft Kinect v2 sensor to represent the spatial features of the signs. We model the temporal aspect of the signs by using Dynamic Time Warping (DTW) and Temporal Templates (TT). Finally, we classify spatio-temporal features extracted from the isolated sign phrases using k-Nearest Neighbours (k-NN) and Random Decision Forest (RDF) classifiers.

We evaluated the performance of the proposed recognition scheme on a subset of the BosphorusSign corpus [3], that contains a total of 1257 samples belonging to 33 signs, which were collected from six native TİD users. We investigated each features effect on the recognition performance and compared temporal modelling and classification approaches. In our experiments, combining hand position and hand movement features achieved the highest recognition performance while both of the temporal modelling and classification approaches yielded satisfactory recognition results. Moreover, we inspected the outcome of using the tree-based activity diagram interaction scheme and came to the conclusion that this approach increases the overall recognition performance.

In Sect. 2, we briefly explain the tree-based activity diagram interaction scheme in HospiSign. Section 3 describes our proposed sign language recognition method. Experimental results are given in Sect. 4 and finally, we conclude the paper in Sect. 5.

2   The Hospital Information System User Interface

The hospital information system user interface provides a communication medium for the hearing impaired in a hospital information desk setting. By asking questions in the form of sign videos and suggesting possible answers on a display, the system helps Deaf users to explain their problems. With the tree-based activity diagram interaction scheme, which can be seen in Fig. 1, the system only looks for the possible answers in each activity group, instead of trying to recognize from all the signs in the database. At the end of the interaction, the system prints out a summary of the interaction and the users are guided to take this print out with their ID to the information desk, where they can be assisted according to their needs.

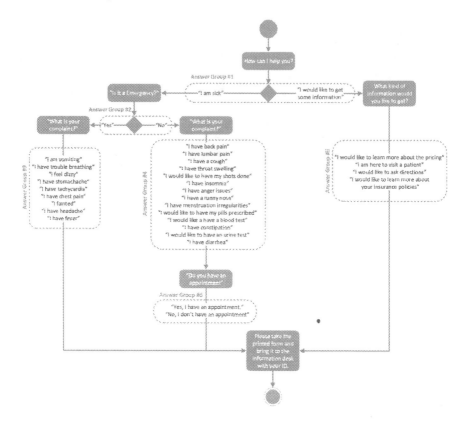

Fig. 1. Tree-based activity diagram interaction scheme of HospiSign.

The HospiSign platform consists of a personal computer, a touch display to visualize the sign questions and answers to the user, and a Microsoft Kinect v2 sensor. Since it is necessary to track the users' hand motions in order to recognize the performed signs, the Microsoft Kinect v2 sensor plays an essential role as it provides accurate real-time human body pose information.

The HospiSign system follows three stages to move from one question to the next in the tree-based activity diagram interaction scheme: (1) display of the question; (2) display of the possible answers to that question; and (3) the recognition of the answer (sign). The user first watches the question displayed on the top-center of the screen; then performs a sign from the list of possible answers displayed at the bottom of the screen, and then moves to the next question. This process is repeated until the system gathers all the necessary information from the user. After the user answers all the required questions, the system prints out a summary report to be given to the information desk or the doctor at the hospital. This summary contains the details of the user's interaction with HospiSign.

To make the classification task easier, the questions are placed into a tree-based activity diagram in such a way that each question will lead to another sub-question with respect to the answer selected by the user. With categorization of possible answers to each question, it is intended to help the users to easily describe their symptoms or intention of their visit.

One of the most important advantages of using such a tree-based scheme is that it makes the system more user-friendly and easy-to-interact. The tree-based activity diagram interaction scheme also increases the recognition speed and performance of the system as the task of recognizing a sign from possible answers to each question is much easier and faster than recognizing a sign from the all possible answers.

3   Proposed Sign Language Recognition Method

The proposed sign language recognition method consists of four modules: Human Pose Estimation, Feature Extraction, Feature Normalization and Selection, and Temporal Modeling and Classification, as visualized in Fig. 2. Taking this framework as a baseline, the usage of various features, their combinations, temporal modeling techniques and classification methods are proposed to represent, and to recognize isolated sign language phrases.

The first step of the recognition module, human pose estimation, is critical since illumination and background variations introduce great challenges. As it uses active projective light imaging, the Microsoft Kinect v2 sensor is able to overcome these challenges. By using its pose estimation library routines, we were able to extract world coordinates, pixel coordinates and orientations of the 25 body joints.

As sign languages convey information through hand shape, upper body pose, facial expressions and hand trajectories, sign language recognition techniques extract features to represent each respective aspect of the signs. Kadir et al. [8] proposed specialized hand position and hand movement features in order to represent signs and capture their distinguishing properties. The features consist of hand positions and hand movements. Taking these features as baseline,

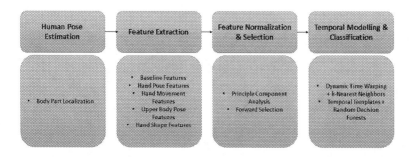

Fig. 2. Four main modules of our sign language recognition framework.

hand position (Baseline Hand Position) and hand movement (Baseline Hand Movement) features were extracted from each video frame to represent sign samples.

In addition, we have extracted upper body pose (Normalized World Coordinates, Normalized Pixel Coordinates, Upper Body Joint Orientations), hand movement (Hand Joint Movement), and hand position (Hand Joint Distance) features using the body pose information provided by Microsoft Kinect v2 sensor.

Normalized World and Pixel Coordinates were extracted from the world and pixel coordinates that were provided by the Microsoft Kinect v2 sensor. The normalization was done by subtracting the Hip Center joint from the upper body joints, that are Head, Shoulder, Elbow, Wrist, Hand and Spine Joints, thus removing the location variance of the users. Then each joint coordinate is divided by the distance between the Shoulder Center and Hip Center joints in y axis, thus removing the scale (users' height) variance. We used Joint Orientation features as it is provided by the Microsoft Kinect v2 sensor.

Hand Joint Distance features were extracted by calculating the euclidean distance between the hand joints and the upper body joints, that were previously mentioned. The normalization of these features was done by dividing each distance by the sum of all Hand Joint Distances in its respective frame. Hand Movement Distance features represent the temporal dislocation of hands between subsequent frames and they were extracted by calculating the distance of each hands location from its location in the previous frame (in x, y, and z axis).

To represent hand shapes, we segmented the hand images using the hand joints' pixel coordinates and the signers' skin colors. We cropped a window of 80*80 pixel around both of the and joints and masked the hand using color based skin detection. Then we extracted Histogram of Oriented Gradients [6] with various Cell and Block Sizes from the segmented hand patches for each frame. A list of our features, the aspects they represent in a sign and their sizes can be seen in Table 1.

Table 1. Extracted features that are used to represent signs.

Feature name	Represented aspect	Feature size
Baseline Hand Positions	Hand Position	27
Baseline Hand Movements	Hand Movement	11
Normalized World Coordinates	Upper Body Pose	36
Normalized Pixel Coordinates	Upper Body Pose	24
Joint Orientations	Upper Body Pose	48
Hand Joint Distances	Hand Position	22
Hand Movement Distances	Hand Movement	6
HOG (L-M-H)	Hand Shape	18-108-432

As different features come from different distributions and have different scales we applied Principal Component Analysis (PCA) [7] to each feature separately before combining them in the temporal modeling and classification steps.

For temporal modeling and classification, we have proposed two approaches. The first approach is to model the temporal aspect of signs using Dynamic Time Warping (DTW) and classify samples using k-Nearest Neighbours (k-NN) algorithm. DTW is a popular tool for finding the optimal alignment between two time series. The DTW algorithm calculates the distance between each possible pair of points in terms of their spatial and temporal features. DTW uses these distances to calculate a cumulative distance matrix and finds the least expensive path through this matrix using dynamic programming. This path represents the ideal synchronization of the two series with the minimal feature distance. Usually, the samples are normalized to zero mean and smoothed with median filtering before distance calculation. The weighting of each feature inversely proportional to their feature size is applied to avoid features with larger sizes suppressing the effectiveness of features with smaller sizes. To classify a sign sample, its distance to the each training sample is calculated and the class of the sign is assigned using k-Nearest Neighbours algorithm.

The second approach is based on Temporal Templates (TT) and Random Decision Forest (RDF). Random Decision Forest is a supervised classification and regression technique that has become widely used due to its efficiency and simplicity. RDFs are an ensemble of random decision trees (RDT) [2]. However, RDFs do not inherently possess a temporal representation scheme. To incorporate the temporal aspect, Temporal Templates (TT), that represent each frame with the concatenated features of its neighbours are used in combination with Random Decision Forests. In template based temporal modelling, increasing template size enhances temporal representation. However, memory and computational power restrictions of development systems limit the feature vector size. To overcome this limitation, we downsample the data with various interval sizes to represent larger temporal windows while using the same number of frames. We classify the constructed temporal template of each frame by using Random Decision Forests (RDFs). Each tree is trained on a randomly sampled subset of the training data. This reduces over-fitting in comparison to training RDFs on the entire database; therefore increasing stability and accuracy. During training, a tree learns to split the original problem into smaller ones. At each non-leaf node, tests are generated through randomly selected subsets of features and thresholds. The tests are scored using the decrease in entropy, and best splits are chosen and used for each node [2]. Each tree ends with leaf nodes, that represent the probabilities of a given data to belong to the possible classes. Classification of a frame is performed by starting at the root node and assigning the frame either to the left or to the right child recursively until a leaf node is reached. Majority voting is used on the prediction of all decision trees to decide on the final class of the frame. Finally, signs are classified by taking the mode of its frames' classification results.

In the Dynamic Time Warping and K-nearest Neighbours based approach we choose the best combination of features by applying a greedy forward search algorithm, in which we iteratively added features by starting from the best performing feature until the recognition performance stopped increasing. There was no need for feature selection for the Temporal Template and Random Decision Forest based approach as the Random Decision Forests weight the features in their training.

4   Experiments and Results

All the experiments were conducted on a subset of the BosphorusSign database, which is used in the development of HospiSign. The subset contains 1257 sign phrase samples belonging to 33 phrase classes which were performed by six native TİD users in six to eight repetitions. In order to obtain user independent results we performed leave-one-user-out cross-validation and report the mean and standard deviation of recognition performance in all of our experiments.

The performance of the implemented methods were examined in terms of the features, temporal modeling techniques, and classification approaches. The first experiments were conducted to find the optimum parameters for Histogram of Oriented Gradients, which was used to represent hand shapes. Three HOG parameter setups were used that are Low Detailed (HOG-L, Cell Size: [80 × 80] Block Size: [1 × 1]), Medium Detailed (HOG-M, Cell Size: [40 × 40] Block Size: [2 × 2]), and High Detailed (HOG-H, Cell Size: [20 × 20] Block Size: [4 × 4]). Examples of all the three parameter setups can be seen in Fig. 3. The parameter optimization results for different users demonstrate that while appearance based features worked well for some users, achieving up to 88 % accuracies, they did not produce reliable classifiers for others. The results can be observed in Table 2. Since HOG-M has the highest accuracy, we used it in the rest of our experiments.

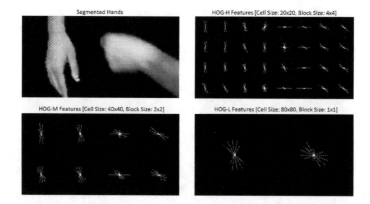

Fig. 3. Segmented hands and extracted Histogram of Oriented Gradients with different parameter setups. Top Left: Segmented Hands, Top Right: HOG-H, Bottom Left: HOG-M, Bottom Right: HOG-L.

Table 2. Recognition performance of different HOG parameters

	User 1	User 2	User 3	User 4	User 5	User 6	Mean ± Std
HOG-H	51.01	47.17	66.83	20.00	20.20	20.60	37.64 ± 20.14
HOG-M	78.28	84.91	86.93	22.00	30.81	26.13	**54.84 ± 31.51**
HOG-L	70.20	82.64	88.44	25.00	23.23	37.19	54.45 ± 29.46

Table 3. Performance evaluation of features

	User 1	User 2	User 3	User 4	User 5	User 6	Mean ± Std
Hand Joint Distances	96.46	94.72	95.98	86.00	86.36	96.98	**92.75 ± 5.15**
Norm. Pixel Coordinates	94.95	93.96	98.49	86.00	83.84	94.97	92.04 ± 5.76
Norm. World Coordinates	94.95	95.85	97.49	85.00	80.30	91.46	90.84 ± 6.81
Hand Movement Distances	90.40	86.79	91.96	83.00	64.65	68.84	80.94 ± 11.50
Baseline Hand Movements	75.76	72.83	81.91	78.50	44.44	68.34	70.30 ± 13.49
Baseline Hand Positions	64.14	75.85	68.34	53.50	55.05	68.34	64.20 ± 8.58
HOG-M	78.28	84.91	86.93	22.00	30.81	26.13	54.84 ± 31.51
Joint Orientations	32.83	38.49	44.72	34.50	26.77	38.69	36.00 ± 6.12
All Features Combined	67,68	77,36	85,93	67,00	47,47	75,38	**70,14 ± 13,10**

By using the best performing HOG setup, we conducted experiments in order to find the combination of features that yield the highest recognition performance. In feature selection experiments Dynamic Time Warping (DTW) was used to measure the distance between isolated sign phrases. Using the distances provided by DTW, k-Nearest Neighbours (k-NN) algorithm was used to classify the isolated signs by taking the mode of its k nearest neighbours' class labels. Table 3 lists the recognition accuracies of individual features for each user. It is observed that Hand Joint Distances yield the highest performance. While some features show comparable performance with the Hand Joint Distances, the rest of the features such as Joint Orientations perform poorly. When all features are combined, average performance drops to 70.14 %.

Even though the performance of some features are inferior, they may have complementary value, and a combination of features may perform better. To see which combination performs better, we have employed forward search. Table 4 shows the first step of forward search: It is observed that the Hand Movement Distances, a dynamic feature, has complementary value and enhances performance. While appearance based features such as HOG contain complementary information, we see that their performance is not consistent across different users. We stop at two features because adding any third feature to the combination of Hand Joint Distances and Hand Movement Distances decreased the recognition performance. Tables 3 and 4 list the performance accuracies of different users separately. It is observed that the performance for User 5 is lower than other users. By inspection of sign videos, we have observed that User 5 performs signs differently: For example, that user performs signs repeatedly and much faster.

Table 4. Forward selection of features combined with Hand Joint Distances feature.

	User 1	User 2	User 3	User 4	User 5	User 6	Mean ± Std
Hand Joint Distances	96.46	94.72	95.98	86.00	86.36	96.98	**92.75 ± 5.15**
Norm. Pixel Coordinates	94.95	94.34	98.49	86.00	84.34	95.48	92.27 ± 5.70
Norm. World Coordinates	95.96	96.23	96.98	85.00	80.30	93.47	91.32 ± 6.98
Hand Movement Distances	96.46	95.09	98.99	91.00	82.32	98.99	**93.81 ± 6.36**
Baseline Hand Movements	87.88	85.28	89.95	89.00	62.12	80.90	82.52 ± 10.51
Baseline Hand Positions	87.88	87.17	94.97	84.50	78.28	91.46	87.38 ± 5.76
HOG-M	95.96	96.23	96.98	84.00	78.79	95.98	91.32 ± 7.87
Joint Orientations	37.88	44.53	51.76	38.50	29.80	42.21	40.78 ± 7.36

Table 5. Temporal Template Size and Interval Steps optimization results. TS: Template Size, IS: Interval Steps.

	IS: 1	IS: 2	IS: 3	IS: 5
TS: 9	84,56 ± 5,65	90,89 ± 4,17	92,94 ± 3,16	95,54 ± 1,87
TS: 11	87,37 ± 6,32	91,77 ± 3,43	94,41 ± 2,13	95,96 ± 1,57
TS: 13	87,91 ± 5,35	93,07 ± 3,41	95,23 ± 2,13	**96,67 ± 1,80**
TS: 15	89,86 ± 4,39	94,26 ± 2,66	95,27 ± 1,95	96,65 ± 2,04
TS: 17	89,86 ± 4,39	94,26 ± 2,66	95,90 ± 2,03	96,38 ± 1,67
TS: 19	90,83 ± 3,57	94,91 ± 1,82	96,19 ± 1,69	96,08 ± 2,28
TS: 21	91,45 ± 3,82	94,91 ± 1,68	96,40 ± 2,03	95,96 ± 3,03
TS: 23	92,69 ± 2,95	95,35 ± 1,73	96,48 ± 2,02	95,22 ± 3,97

One other observation is that in Table 4, while the recognition performance of Normalized Pixel and World Coordinates and HOG-M increases performance for Users 2 and 3 who are expert level signers, they decrease significantly for Users 4 and 5 who show variations in their performance with respect to speed and sign positions.

Then we conduct experiments in order to find the optimum window size and interval steps (down-sampling rate) for the Temporal Templates (TT). We classify the Temporal Templates using Random Decision Forest (RDF) that contains 100 trees.

As it can be seen in Table 5, as the template size and interval steps increase, the recognition performance also gets better until an optimum size of represented temporal window. While lower template sizes benefit from higher interval steps, this trend is lost with higher template sizes. We choose a template size of 13 and down-sampling rate(interval step) of 5 since that yields the best performance.

In the light of our experiments, we have seen that DTW and RDF reach 93.81 % and 96, 67 % average recognition accuracies respectively on 33 classes of signs of six different users in leave-one-user-out cross-validation tests. However, in HospiSign, the tree-based activity diagram interaction scheme, that is displayed in Fig. 1, guides its users to perform signs from a limited subset at each step.

Table 6. Mean and standard deviation of recognition results of DTW and RDF based methods with and without the Activity Diagram based recognition scheme

Setup	nClasses	DTW+k-NN	TT+RDF	Combined
All Signs	33	93.81 ± 6.36	96,67 ± 1,80	N/A
Activity Group 1	2	100.00 ± 0.00	100.00 ± 0.00	100.00 ± 0.00
Activity Group 2	2	100.00 ± 0.00	100.00 ± 0.00	100.00 ± 0.00
Activity Group 3	9	100.00 ± 0.00	98,78 ± 1.53	100.00 ± 0.00
Activity Group 4	14	95.86 ± 3.05	97,88 ± 1,67	97.88 ± 1.67
Activity Group 5	4	97.92 ± 5.1	98,09 ± 3,39	98,09 ± 3,39
Activity Group 6	2	100.00 ± 0.00	100.00 ± 0.00	100.00 ± 0.00

We have conducted experiments using the best performing parameters for both the DTW+k-NN and TT+RDF based approaches and reported the results in Table 6.

As the number of classes that the systems requires to classify from decreases, the recognition performance improves drastically. Moreover, as each activity group in the tree-based activity diagram interaction scheme is a different recognition task, we can combine the best performing temporal modeling and classification approaches, thus further increasing the recognition performance. By choosing the best performing approach for each activity group, we have achieved 100 % recognition performance for four activity groups and more than 97.88 % recognition performance for the renaming two activity groups, suppressing the best recognition performance of recognizing signs from 33 classes (96.67 % using TT+RDF approach). The reason that the two activity groups that hand lower recognition performance then the rest is the similarity of signs in Activity Group 4 (All of phrases are ending in the same way) and the larger number of classes that system is required to be classified from in Activity Group 5 (14 sign phrase classes).

5   Conclusion

In this study, a real time sign language recognition system was designed with the aim of working as a communication platform for a hospital information desk. The system was developed using a Microsoft Kinect v2 sensor to aid with the human pose estimation. The recognition system, trained with a subset of the Bosphorus-Sign database [3], extracts hand shape, hand position, hand movement and upper body pose features and performs temporal modelling using Dynamic Time Warping and Temporal Templates. The spatio-temporally represented signs are then classified using k-Nearest Neighbours algorithm and Random Decision Forests.

The experiments demonstrate that the highest recognition (93.81 %) was achieved by using the Hand Joint Distance and Hand Movement Distance features while using the Dynamic Time Warping and k-Nearest Neighbours based recognition approach. These features were selected using a greedy forward selection scheme. Forward selection demonstrated that the presence of any other feature reduced overall recognition performance for all users. However, it is interesting to note that while appearance and coordinate based features performed well with recognition from three users, they were not effective with other users who performed the signs with more variation in location and speed. This can be explained by the fact that while these features do posses complementary information that may be helpful in recognition, their variation among different users makes them user and recording environment dependent. This is especially important when designing an online recognition system such as HospiSign, as the system becomes more robust the less it is over-trained on users who perform the signs perfectly with little room for variations.

In the experiments, in which the signs were temporally modeled using Temporal Templates and classified using Random Decision Forests, the best recognition performance (96.67 %) was achieved using a template size of 13 with interval steps of 5. As the Random Decision Forests does the feature selection in its training, no additional feature selection scheme was applied in these experiments.

Our experiments demonstrate that while using the 33 class classification scheme the highest recognition performance (96.67 %) was achieved by using the Temporal Template and Random Decision Forest based classification approach. However, by using the tree-based activity diagram interaction scheme, we were able to improve the recognition performance for all of the activity groups, as the systems has to recognize signs from a lower number of classes in each step of the interaction. One of the main benefits of using the tree-based activity diagram interaction scheme is that the best performing approaches can be used for the classification of each activity group. By combining the best performing classification approach for each activity group, we were able to reach 100 % recognition performance in four activity groups and more then 97.88 % recognition performance for the remaining two activity groups, thus suppressing the recognition performance of 96.67 %.

References

1. Berndt, D., Clifford, J.: Using dynamic time warping to find patterns in time series. In: Workshop on Knowledge Knowledge Discovery in Databases, vol. 398, pp. 359–370 (1994)
2. Breiman, L.: Random forests. Mach. Learn. **45**(5), 1–35 (1999)
3. Camgöz, N.C., Kindiroglu, A.A., Karabüklü, S., Kelepir, M., Akarun, L., Ozsoy, S.: BosphorusSign: a Turkish sign language recognition corpus in health and finance domains. In: LREC (2016)
4. Chai, X., Li, G., Chen, X., Zhou, M., Wu, G., Li, H.: VisualComm: a tool to support communication between deaf and hearing persons with the Kinect. In: Proceedings of the 15th International ACM SIGACCESS Conference on Computers and Accessibility (2013)
5. Cox, S., Lincoln, M., Tryggvason, J.: TESSA, a system to aid communication with deaf people. In: Proceedings of the Fifth International ACM Conference on Assistive Technologies. ACM (2002)

6. Dalal, N., Triggs, B.: Histogram of oriented gradients for human detection. In: 2005 IEEE Computer Society Conference on Computer Vision and Pattern Recognition, CVPR 2005, vol. 1, pp. 886–893 (2005)
7. Jolliffe, I.: Principal Component Analysis. Wiley Online Library, Chichester (2002)
8. Kadir, T., Bowden, R., Ong, E., Zisserman, A.: Minimal training, large lexicon, unconstrained sign language recognition. In: British Machine Vision Conference (2004)
9. Kose, H., Yorganci, R., Algan, E.H., Syrdal, D.S.: Evaluation of the robot assisted sign language tutoring using video-based studies. Int. J. Social Robot. **4**(3), 273–283 (2012)
10. Lee, H., Kim, J.: An HMM-based threshold model approach for gesture recognition. IEEE Trans. Pattern Anal. Mach. Intell. **21**(10), 961–973 (1999)
11. Lopez-Ludena, V., Gonzalez-Morcillo, C., Lopez, J.C., Barra-Chicote, R., Cordoba, R., San-Segundo, R.: Translating bus information into sign language for deaf people. Eng. Appl. Artif. Intell. **32**, 258–269 (2014)
12. Ong, S.C.W., Ranganath, S.: Automatic sign language analysis: a survey and the future beyond lexical meaning. IEEE Trans. Pattern Anal. Mach. Intell. **27**(6), 873–91 (2005)
13. Pitsikalis, V., Theodorakis, S., Vogler, C., Maragos, P.: Advances in phonetics-based sub-unit modeling for transcription alignment and sign language recognition. In: IEEE Computer Society Conference on Computer Vision and Pattern Recognition Workshops (2011)
14. Rabiner, L., Juang, B.: An introduction to hidden Markov models. ASSP Magazine, IEEE (1986)
15. Shotton, J., Fitzgibbon, A., Cook, M., Sharp, T., Finocchio, M., Moore, R., Kipman, A., Blake, A.: Real-time human pose recognition in parts from single depth images. In: CVPR, vol. 2 (2011)
16. Starner, T., Pentland, A.: Real-time American sign language recognition from video using hidden Markov models. In: 1995 Proceedings of the Computer Vision (1995)
17. Süzgün, M.M., Özdemir, H., Camgöz, N.C., Kindiroglu, A.A., Başaran, D., Togay, C., Akarun, L.: HospiSign: an interactive sign language platform for hearing impaired. In: Proceedings - Eurasia Graphics 2015, Istanbul (2015)
18. Theodorakis, S., Pitsikalis, V., Maragos, P.: Dynamic-static unsupervised sequentiality, statistical subunits and lexicon for sign language recognition. Image Vis. Comput. **32**, 533–549 (2014)
19. Vogler, C., Metaxas, D.: Parallel hidden Markov models for American sign language recognition. In: Proceedings of the Seventh IEEE International Conference on Computer Vision, vol. 1, pp. 116–122 (1999)
20. Weaver, K.a., Starner, T.: We Need to Communicate! Helping Hearing Parents of Deaf Children Learn American Sign Language. Assets (Xiii), p. 91 (2011)
21. Yorganci, R., Akalin, N., Kose, H.: Avatar Tabanlı Etkileşimli İşaret Dili Oyunları. In: Uluslararası Engelsiz Bilişim 2015 Kongresi. Manisa (2015)
22. Zhang, Z.: Microsoft Kinect sensor and its effect. IEEE Multimedia **19**(2), 4–10 (2012)

Using the Audio Respiration Signal
for Multimodal Discrimination
of Expressive Movement Qualities

Vincenzo Lussu, Radoslaw Niewiadomski$^{(\boxtimes)}$, Gualtiero Volpe,
and Antonio Camurri

Casa Paganini - InfoMus, DIBRIS - University of Genoa,
Viale Francesco Causa 13, 16145 Genoa, Italy
radoslaw.niewiadomski@dibris.unige.it, gualtiero.Volpe@unige.it

Abstract. In this paper we propose a multimodal approach to distinguish between movements displaying three different expressive qualities:
fluid, fragmented, and impulsive movements. Our approach is based on
the Event Synchronization algorithm, which is applied to compute the
amount of synchronization between two low-level features extracted from
multimodal data. In more details, we use the energy of the audio respiration signal captured by a standard microphone placed near to the mouth,
and the whole body kinetic energy estimated from motion capture data.
The method was evaluated on 90 movement segments performed by 5
dancers. Results show that fragmented movements display higher average synchronization than fluid and impulsive movements.

Keywords: Movement analysis · Expressive qualities · Respiration ·
Synchronization

1 Introduction

Expressive qualities of movement refer to how a movement is performed. The
same movement can be performed with different qualities, e.g., in a fluid, fragmented, hesitant, impulsive, or contracted way. Expressive qualities are a very
relevant aspect of dance, where e.g., they convey emotion to external observers.
They also play an important role in rehabilitation, sport, and entertainment
(e.g., in video-games). Several computational models and analysis techniques for
assessing and measuring expressive movement qualities have been proposed (see
e.g., [14] for a recent review), as well as algorithms to automatically detect and
compute expressive qualities of a movement (e.g., [2]). In this paper, we propose
a multimodal approach to analysis of expressive qualities of movement, integrating respiration and movement data. Whilst motion capture systems, often used
to analyze human behavior, provide precise and accurate data on human motion,
they are very invasive and cannot be used in several scenarios e.g., in artistic
performance. In the long term, the multimodal technique discussed here for distinguishing between expressive qualities may make the use of motion capture
systems dispensable.

© Springer International Publishing AG 2016
M. Chetouani et al. (Eds.): HBU 2016, LNCS 9997, pp. 102–115, 2016.
DOI: 10.1007/978-3-319-46843-3_7

Respiration is of paramount importance for body movement. Respiration is strongly related to any physical activity. The interaction between body movement and respiration is bidirectional. The respiration pattern may provoke certain visible body movements, e.g., in the case of laughter [15]. It can also be influenced by body movements, e.g., huddling oneself up corresponds to the expiration phase. Rhythm of respiration synchronizes with repetitive motoric activities such as running [8]. Several physical activities such as yoga or tai-chi explicitly connect physical movement to respiration patterns. In this work dance is taken as a use case. During a dance performance, dancers are used to display a huge variety of expressive qualities, and they dedicate a lot of effort and time to exercise their expressive vocabulary. Thus, one can expect that various performances by the same dancer, conveying different expressive qualities, can provide a solid ground to base our study upon.

In this paper, we hypothesize that different multimodal synchronization patterns can be observed for movements performed with different expressive qualities. Movements displaying different qualities such as fluid, fragmented, or impulsive movements engage different parts of the body to different extents. For example, whilst fluid movements are propagated along the kinematic chains of the body, impulsive and fragmented movements usually engage most of the body parts at once. Consequently, respiration patterns may be influenced by the expressive quality of movement. To confirm our hypothesis, we study intrapersonal synchronization between two features, one extracted from the audio signal of respiration and one from motion capture data.

The paper is organized as follows: in Sect. 2, we present existing works on analysis of human movement and of respiration signals; in Sect. 3, we describe the expressive qualities we study in this paper; Sect. 4 presents our dataset; Sect. 5 describes the techniques we developed and tested in the experiment presented in Sect. 6; we conclude the paper in Sect. 7.

2   State of the Art

Several works analyzed respiration in sport activities such as walking and running [4,8], and rowing [3]. Respiration data was also used to detect emotions [11]. Bernasconi and Kohl [4] studied the effect of synchronization between respiration rhythm and legs movement rhythm to analyze efficiency in physical activities such as running or cycling. They measured synchronization as a percentage of the coincidence between the beginning of a respiration phase and the beginning of a step (or a pedaling cycle). According to their results, the higher is synchronization the higher is efficiency and the lower is consumption of oxygen.

Bateman and colleagues [3] measured synchronization between the start of a respiration phase, and the phase of a stroke in rowing by expert and non-expert rowers. Respiration phases were detected with a nostril thermistor, whereas the stroke phase (1 out of 4) was detected from the spinal kinematics and the force applied to the rowing machine. The higher synchronization the higher stroke rate was observed for expert rowers. Additionally, the most frequently observed pattern consisted of two breath cycles per stroke.

Schmid and colleagues [22] analyzed synchronization between postural sway and respiration patterns captured with a respiratory belt at chest level. A difference was observed in respiration frequency and amplitude between sitting and standing position.

In most of the works that consider respiration, data is captured with respiration sensors such as belt-like strips placed on the chest, or other very dedicated devices. An example of such a device is the CO2100C module by Biopac[1] that measures the quantity of CO_2 in the exhaled air. This sensor is able to detect even very short changes of carbon dioxide concentration levels. Unfortunately, this method is very invasive, thus several alternative solutions were proposed (see [7,20] for recent reviews). Folke and colleagues [7] proposed three major categories of measurements for the respiration signal:

– movement, volume, and tissue composition measurements, e.g., transthoracic impedance measured with skin electrodes placed on chest;
– air flow measurements, e.g., nasal thermistors;
– blood gas concentration measurements, e.g., the pulse - oximetry method that measures oxygen saturation in blood.

Several works focused on tracheal signals. Huq and colleagues [9] distinguished the respiration phases using the average power and log-variance of the band-pass filtered tracheal breath. In particular, the strongest differences between the two respiratory phases were found in the 300–450 Hz and 800–1000 Hz bands for average power and log-variance respectively. Jin and colleagues [10] segmented breath using tracheal signals through genetic algorithms.

Another popular approach is to use Inertial Measurement Units (IMUs). In [13] a single IMU sensor was placed on the person's abdomen and it was used to extract the respiration pattern. The raw signal captured with the IMU device was filtered with an adaptive filter based on energy expenditure (EE) to remove frequencies that are not related to respiration. Three classes of activities were considered: Low EE (e.g., sitting) Medium EE (e.g., walking), and High EE (e.g., running).

Some works used the audio signal of respiration captured with a microphone placed near the mouth. In [1], the audio of respiration was used to detect the respiration phases. For this purpose, authors first isolated the respiration segments using a Voice Activity Detection (VAD) algorithm based on short time energy (STE). Next, they computed Mel-frequency cepstrum coefficients (MFCC) of respiration segments, and they used MFCC and a linear thresholding to distinguish between the two respiration phases. Yahya and colleagues [23] also classified respiration phases from audio data. Again, a VAD algorithm was applied to the audio signal to extract the respiration segments. Next several low-level audio features extracted from the segments were used by a Support Vector Machine (SVM) classifier to separate the exhilaration segments from the inspiration ones.

Ruinskiy and colleagues [21] aimed to separate respiration segments from voice segments in audio recordings. First, they created a respiration template

---

[1] http://www.biopac.com/.

using a mean cepstrogram matrix for each participant. Next they used it to compute a similarity measurement between the template and an input segment in order to classify the input segment as a breathy/not breathy one.

Compared to the state-of-the-art, this work brings the following contributions:

- according to the authors' knowledge, this is the first work that uses information extracted from the respiration data to distinguish between different expressive qualities of movement,
- contrary to most of previous works, we use a standard microphone to study respiration and we capture respiration data from the microphone placed near to the mouth. This approach is appropriate to capture e.g., dancers respiration patterns, because dancers do not speak during a performance, but they move a lot and cannot wear invasive devices. Our approach is less invasive than other approaches based on other respiration sensors.

3   Definitions of Expressive Qualities

Recently, Camurri and colleagues [5] proposed a conceptual framework conceived for analysis of expressive content conveyed by whole body movement and gesture. The framework consists of four layers: the first one is responsible for capturing and preprocessing data from sensor systems, including video, motion capture, and audio. The second one computes low-level motion features such as *energy* or *smoothness* at a small time scale (i.e., frame by frame or over short time windows e.g., 100 ms–150 ms long) from such data. The third layer computes mid-level features such as *fluidity, impulsivity*, and so on, i.e., complex higher-level qualities that are usually extracted on groups of joints or on the whole body, and require significantly longer temporal intervals to be detected (i.e., 0.5 s–3 s). Finally, the fourth layer corresponds to even higher-level communicative expressive qualities, such as the user's emotional states and social attitudes. Following this framework, in this paper we focus on three expressive movement qualities belonging to the third layer, i.e., fluid, fragmented, and impulsive movements. These three qualities at layer 3 are modeled in terms of features at layers 1 and 2. Below, we recall the definitions of these qualities.

Fluid Movement. A *fluid movement* is characterized by the following properties [18]:

- the movement of each involved body joint is smooth;
- the energy of movement (energy of muscles) is free to propagate along the kinematic chains of (parts of) the body according to a coordinated wave-like propagation.

Fluidity is a major expressive quality in classical dance and ballet. Outside the dance context, fluid movements are, for example, body movements as in the butterfly swimming technique, or moving as a fish in the water.

Fragmented Movement. A *fragmented movement* is characterized by:

- non coordinated propagation of energy between adjacent body joints, i.e., only "bursts" of propagation are observed;
- autonomous movements of different parts of the body, i.e., autonomous and non (or lowly) correlated sequences of "free" followed by "bound" movements (in Laban's Effort terms [12]): typically, a joint alternates a free movement (e.g., for a short time interval) with a "bound" movement;
- joints movements are neither synchronized nor coordinated among themselves: an observer perceives the whole body movement as composed by parts of the body obeying to separate and independent motor planning strategies, with no unified, coherent, and harmonic global movement.

Such movements are typical, for example, in contemporary dance.

Impulsive Movement. An *impulsive movement* is characterized by [16]:

- a sudden and non predictable change of velocity;
- no preparation phase.

Examples of impulsive movements are avoidance movements (e.g., when hearing a sudden and unexpected noise) or a movement to recover from a loss of balance. It is important to notice that impulsivity is different from high kinetic energy. Quick but repetitive movements are not impulsive.

4 Experimental Setup

We collected a set of short performances of dancers asked to perform whole body movements with a requested expressive quality. Five female dancers were invited to participate in the recordings. They performed short performances focusing on one of the three selected expressive qualities. Each trial had a duration of 1.5 to 2 min. At the beginning of each session, dancers were given definitions of the expressive quality by means of textual images (more details on the recording procedure are available in [17]). The dancers were asked to perform: (i) an improvised choreography containing movements that, in their opinion, express the quality convincingly, as well as (ii) several repetitions of predefined sequences of movements by focusing on the given expressive quality.

A custom procedure was defined to obtain and record several impulsive movements: the blindfolded dancer was induced to express this quality by an external event (e.g., an unexpected touch). When she perceived a touch on her body, she had to imagine that she was touched by a hot stick that she had to avoid. Thus, for impulsive trials, the dancer was, by default, performing fluid movements and impulsive movements appears only when she is touched (for more details see [17]). Each quality was performed by two different dancers.

We recorded multimodal data captured with (i) a Qualisys motion capture system, tracking 6 single markers and 11 rigid bodies (10 on the body and 1 on the head) plates at 100 frames per second; resulting data consists of the 3D positions of 60 markers; (ii) one wireless microphone (mono, 48 kHz) placed close to the dancer's mouth, recording the sound of respiration; (iii) 2 video cameras (1280×720, at 50 fps).

The freely available EyesWeb XMI platform, developed at University of Genoa[2], was used for synchronized recording and analysis of the multimodal streams of data. Motion capture data was cleaned, missing data was filled using linear and polynomial interpolation.

5   Analysis Techniques

Our aim is to check whether the overall amount of synchronization between low-level features from movement and from the audio signal of respiration enable us to distinguish between the three selected expressive qualities. In more details, we consider one audio feature: the energy of the audio signal, and one movement feature: the kinetic energy of the whole body movement. These features were chosen as they can be easily computed in real-time. In the future, we plan to estimate kinetic energy with sensors, which are less invasive than a motion capture system, such as IMUs. We define events to be extracted from the time-series of the low-level features and then we apply the Event Synchronization algorithm [19] to compute the amount of synchronization between the events detected in the two energy time-series. Figure 1 shows the details of our approach.

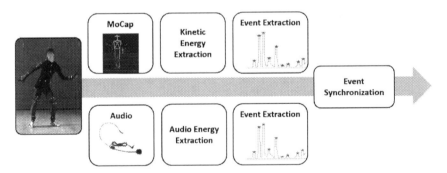

Fig. 1. Block diagram of the analysis procedure. Event Synchronization takes as input events detected in the time-series of energy of the audio signal of respiration and in the time-series of kinetic energy from motion capture data.

5.1   Feature Extraction

The audio signal was segmented in frames of 1920 samples. To synchronize the motion capture data with the audio signal, the former was undersampled at 25 fps. Next, body and audio features were computed separately at this sampling rate.

---

[2] http://www.infomus.org/eyesweb_ita.php.

Motion Capture. Motion capture data was used to compute one movement feature: kinetic energy. This feature was computed in two stages: first, 17 markers from the initial set of 60 were used to compute the instantaneous kinetic energy frame-by-frame. The velocities of single body markers contribute to the instantaneous kinetic energy according to the relative weight of the corresponding body parts as retrieved in anthropometric tables [6]. In the second step, the envelope of the instantaneous kinetic energy was extracted using an 8-frames buffer.

Respiration. The instantaneous energy of the audio signal was computed using Root Mean Square (RMS). This returns one value for every input frame. Next, we extracted the envelope of the instantaneous audio energy using an 8-frames buffer.

5.2   Synchronization

The Event Synchronization (ES) algorithm, proposed by Quian Quiroga and colleagues [19], is used to measure synchronization between two time series in which some events are identified. Let us consider two time-series of features: x_1 and x_2. For each time-series x_i let us define t^{x_i} as the time occurrences of events in x_i. Thus, $t_j^{x_i}$ is the time of the j-th event in time-series x_i. Let m_{x_i} be the number of events in x_i. Then, the amount of synchronization Q^τ is computed as:

$$Q^\tau = \frac{c^\tau(x_1|x_2) + c^\tau(x_2|x_1)}{\sqrt{m_{x_1} m_{x_2}}} \tag{1}$$

where

$$c^\tau(x_1|x_2) = \sum_{i=1}^{m_{x_1}} \sum_{j=1}^{m_{x_2}} J_{ij}^\tau \tag{2}$$

and

$$J_{ij}^\tau = \begin{cases} 1 & if \quad 0 < t_i{}^{x_1} - t_j{}^{x_2} < \tau \\ 1/2 & if \quad t_i{}^{x_1} = t_j{}^{x_2} \\ 0 & otherwise \end{cases} \tag{3}$$

τ defines the length of the synchronization window. Thus, events contribute to the overall amount of synchronization, only if they occur in a τ-long window.

In order to apply the ES algorithm to our data, two steps were needed: (i) defining and retrieving events in our two time-series, and (ii) tuning the parameters of the ES algorithm.

Events Definition. We defined as events the peaks (local maxima) of kinetic and audio energy. To extract peaks, we applied a peak detector algorithm that computes the position of peaks in an N-size buffer, given a threshold α defining the minimal relative "altitude" of a peak. That is, at time p, the local maximum

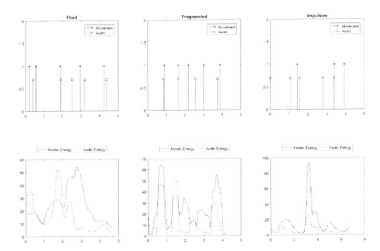

Fig. 2. Three excerpts of the two time-series of energy (audio energy and kinetic energy), representing an example of fluid, fragmented, and impulsive movement respectively (lower panel), and the events extracted from the two time-series and provided as input to the ES algorithm (upper panel).

x_p is considered a peak if the preceding and the following local maxima x_i and x_j are such that $x_i + \alpha < x_p$ and $x_j + \alpha < x_p$, $i < p < j$, and there is no other local maximum x_k, such that $i < k < j$. We empirically chose the buffer size to be 10 frames (corresponding to 400ms) and $\alpha = 0.4465$. Figure 2 shows three excerpts of the two time-series, representing an example of fluid, fragmented, and impulsive movement respectively, and the events the peak detector extracted.

Algorithm Tuning. Next, the ES algorithm was applied to the events identified in the previous step. At each execution, the ES algorithm works on a sliding window of the data and it computes one value – the amount of synchronization Q^τ. In our case, the value of ES is reset at every sliding window. Thus, the past values of ES do not affect the current output. The algorithm has two parameters: the size of the sliding window dim_{sw} and τ. The size of the sliding window was set to 20 samples (corresponding to 800 ms at 25 fps). This value was chosen as the breath frequency of a moving human is in between 35 and 45 cycles per minute. Thus, 800 ms corresponds to half of one breath. We analyzed multimodal synchronization with all τ in interval $[4, dim_{sw} * 0.5]$ (i.e., not higher than half of the size of the sliding window dim_{sw}).

6   Data Analysis and Results

To check whether our approach can distinguish between the three selected expressive qualities, we analyzed the data described in Sect. 4. Our hypothesis is: there are significant differences in the synchronization between the peaks of energy in respiration audio and body movement among the three expressive qualities. At the same time, we expect that there is no significant difference in the synchronization between the peaks of energy in respiration audio and body movement among the different dancers within one single expressive quality. We describe the details below.

6.1   Dataset

Two experts in the domain of expressive movement analysis segmented the data. They selected segments where only one out of the three expressive qualities was clearly observable. Thus, segmentation was based not only on the dancer's expressive intention, but also on the observer's perception of the expressive quality the dancer displayed. Additionally, it was checked whether the audio segments contained only the respiration sounds (segments should not contain any noise that may occasionally occur during the recordings e.g., by unintentionally touching the microphone). The resulting dataset is composed of 90 segments[3] of multimodal data by five dancers. Total duration is 9 min and 20 s. Segments are grouped into three sets, according to the expressive quality they display:

- Fluid Movements Set (*FluidMS*) consisting of 15 segments by Dancer 1 and 15 segments by Dancer 2 (average segment duration 7.615 s, sd = 3.438 s);
- Fragmented Movements Set (*FragMS*) consisting of 15 segments by Dancer 3 and 15 segments by Dancer 4 (average segment duration 5.703 s, sd = 2.519 s);
- Impulsive Movements Set (*ImplMS*) consisting of 15 segments by Dancer 1 and 15 segments by Dancer 5 (average segment duration 5.360 s, sd = 1.741 s).

Due to the complexity of the recording procedure, at the moment we do not have data of one single dancer performing movements displaying all the three expressive qualities. To limit the effect of the particular dancer's personal style we use, for each quality, segments performed by two different dancers.

6.2   Results

For each segment and each considered value of τ, we computed the average value ($AvgQ^\tau$) of the amount of synchronization Q^τ on the whole segment. Next, we computed the mean and standard deviation of $AvgQ^\tau$ separately for all fluid, fragmented, and impulsive segments (see the 4th column of Tables 1, 2 and 3).

To check for differences between the amount of synchronization in the segments in *FluidMS*, *FragMS*, and *ImplMS*, we applied ANOVA with one independent variable, *Quality*, and one dependent variable, $AvgQ^\tau$. All post hoc comparisons were carried out by using the LSD test with Bonferroni correction. Similar results were obtained for all the tested τ. A significant main effect of *Quality* for $\tau = 4$ was observed, $F(2, 87) = 10.973, p < .001$. Post hoc comparisons indicated that multimodal synchronization in fragmented movements was significantly higher compared to the impulsive ($p < .01$), and fluid

---

[3] An example of a segment can be found at: https://youtu.be/J-AtKo2BZ4E.

Table 1. Mean and standard deviation of $AvgQ^\tau$ for fluid movements.

τ	Dancer 1	Dancer 2	Total
$\tau = 4$	0.185 (0.090)	0.188 (0.135)	0.187 (0.113)
$\tau = 6$	0.284 (0.121)	0.298 (0.165)	0.291 (0.143)
$\tau = 8$	0.352 (0.124)	0.378 (0.153)	0.365 (0.138)
$\tau = 10$	0.392 (0.116)	0.419 (0.160)	0.406 (0.137)

Table 2. Mean and standard deviation of $AvgQ^\tau$ for fragmented movements.

τ	Dancer 3	Dancer 4	Total
$\tau = 4$	0.415 (0.186)	0.292 (0.123)	0.354 (0.167)
$\tau = 6$	0.512 (0.191)	0.395 (0.134)	0.454 (0.173)
$\tau = 8$	0.552 (0.170)	0.438 (0.111)	0.495 (0.153)
$\tau = 10$	0.590 (0.167)	0.473 (0.105)	0.532 (0.149)

Table 3. Mean and standard deviation of $AvgQ^\tau$ for impulsive movements.

τ	Dancer 1	Dancer 5	Total
$\tau = 4$	0.241 (0.191)	0.208 (0.093)	0.225 (0.149)
$\tau = 6$	0.353 (0.171)	0.292 (0.095)	0.323 (0.139)
$\tau = 8$	0.379 (0.180)	0.394 (0.106)	0.387 (0.145)
$\tau = 10$	0.425 (0.147)	0.437 (0.111)	0.431 (0.128)

ones ($p < .001$). A significant main effect of $Quality$ for $\tau = 6$ was also observed, $F(2, 87) = 9.650, p < .001$. Post hoc comparisons showed that multimodal synchronization in fragmented movements was significantly higher than in impulsive ($p < .01$), and fluid ones ($p < .001$). A significant main effect of $Quality$ for $\tau = 8$ was also observed, $F(2, 87) = 6.903, p < .01$. Post hoc comparisons indicated that multimodal synchronization in fragmented movements was significantly higher compared to the impulsive ($p < .05$), and fluid ones ($p < .01$). A significant main effect of $Quality$ for $\tau = 10$ was also observed, $F(2, 87) = 6.929, p < .01$. Post hoc comparisons indicated again that multimodal synchronization in fragmented movements was significantly higher compared to the impulsive ($p < .05$), and fluid ones ($p < .01$).

Next, for each $Quality$ and each τ we checked whether there are significant differences between the dancers using independent samples t-tests. Similar results were found for most of the τ values (see Tables 1, 2 and 3). For $\tau = 4$, there was no significant difference for the $FluidMS$ segments (two tailed, $t = -.083$, $df = 28$, $p = .934$), and for the $ImplMS$ segments (two tailed, $t = .600$, $df = 28$, $p = .553$). A significant difference between the two dancers was only observed for the $FragMS$ segments (two tailed, $t = 2.151$, $df = 24.26$, $p < .05$, corrected

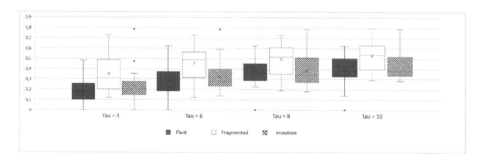

Fig. 3. Box plots of the amount of synchronization for fluid, fragmented, and impulsive movements, respectively.

because of significance of the Levene's test). For $\tau = 6$, no significant differences were observed (*FluidMS*: two tailed, $t = -.267$, $df = 28$, $p = .791$; *ImplMS*: two tailed, $t = 1.200$, $df = 28$, $p = .233$; *FragMS*: two tailed, $t = 1.950$, $df = 28$, $p = .061$). For $\tau = 8$, there was no significant difference between dancers for the *FluidMS* segments (two tailed, $t = -.498$, $df = 28$, $p = .623$), and for the *ImplMS* segments (two tailed, $t = .288$, $df = 28$, $p = .775$). A significant difference between the two dancers was, however, observed for the *FragMS* segments (two tailed, $t = 2.193$, $df = 28$, $p < .05$). For $\tau = 10$, there was no significant difference neither for the *FluidMS* segments (two tailed, $t = -.546$, $df = 28$, $p = .589$), nor for the *ImplMS* ones (two tailed, $t = -.247$, $df = 28$, $p = .807$). A significant difference between the two dancers was observed for the *FragMS* segments (two tailed, $t = 2.303$, $df = 28$, $p < .05$).

6.3   Discussion

According to the results, our hypothesis was confirmed as multimodal synchronization between the energy of the audio signal of respiration and the kinetic energy of whole body movement allowed us to distinguish between the selected expressive qualities. In particular, audio respiration and kinetic energy were found to be more synchronized in fragmented movements than in impulsive and fluid movements. There was no significant difference between impulsive and fluid movements. This might be due to the type of exercise we asked the dancers to perform. In most impulsive segments, dancers were asked to perform one impulsive movement (e.g., when they get touched) while they were moving in a fluid way. Thus, even if the impulsive segments were rather short, it cannot be excluded that the average amount of synchronization in impulsive movements was also affected by the dancer's fluid movements performed before and after the impulsive reaction to the external stimulus.

Significant differences between dancers were found only for fragmented movements. It should be noticed, however, that in the case of fragmented movements the average amount of synchronization for any out of 2 considered dancers was much higher than the average synchronization values for any other quality and dancer.

7   Conclusion and Future Work

In this paper, we proposed a novel approach for distinguishing between expressive qualities of movement from multimodal data, consisting of features from the audio signal of respiration and from body movement. According to the results, our technique – based on the Event Synchronization algorithm – was successful in distinguishing between fragmented and other movements.

This is ongoing work: our long-term aim is to detect different expressive qualities without using a motion capture system. For this purpose, we plan to use data from IMU sensors placed on the dancer's limbs, and to estimate her kinetic energy (and possible further features) using these input devices. This would allow us to eliminate the need of using motion capture systems. At the same time, we want to extract from audio more precise information about the respiration phase. We also plan to study further audio features e.g., MFCC, that proved successful in detection of respiration phases [1].

The results of this work will be exploited in the framework of the EU-H2020 ICT Project DANCE[4], which aims at investigating how sound and music can express, represent, and analyze the affective and relational qualities of body movement. To transfer vision into sound, however, models and techniques are needed to understand what we see when we observe the expressive qualities of a movement. The work presented here is a step toward multimodal analysis of expressive qualities of movement and is propaedeutic to their multi- and cross-sensorial translation.

Acknowledgments. This research has received funding from the European Union's Horizon 2020 research and innovation programme under grant agreement No 645553 (DANCE). DANCE investigates how affective and relational qualities of body movement can be expressed, represented, and analyzed by the auditory channel.

We thank our collegues at Casa Paganini - InfoMus Paolo Alborno, Corrado Canepa, Paolo Coletta, Nicola Ferrari, Simone Ghisio, Maurizio Mancini, Alberto Massari, Ksenia Kolykhalova, Stefano Piana, and Roberto Sagoleo for the fruitful discussions and for their invaluable contributions in the design of the multimodal recordings, and the dancers Roberta Messa, Federica Loredan, and Valeria Puppo for their kind availability to participate in the recordings of our repository of movement qualities.

References

1. Abushakra, A., Faezipour, M.: Acoustic signal classification of breathing movements to virtually aid breath regulation. IEEE J. Biomed. Health Inf. **17**(2), 493–500 (2013)

2. Alborno, P., Piana, S., Mancini, M., Niewiadomski, R., Volpe, G., Camurri, A.: Analysis of intrapersonal synchronization in full-body movements displaying different expressive qualities. In: Proceedings of the International Working Conference on Advanced Visual Interfaces, AVI 2016, New York, pp. 136–143 (2016). http://doi.acm.org/10.1145/2909132.2909262

---

[4] http://dance.dibris.unige.it.

3. Bateman, A., McGregor, A., Bull, A., Cashman, P., Schroter, R.: Assessment of the timing of respiration during rowing and its relationship to spinal kinematics. Biol. Sport **23**, 353–365 (2006)
4. Bernasconi, P., Kohl, J.: Analysis of co-ordination between breathing and exercise rhythms in man. J. Physiol. **471**, 693–706 (1993)
5. Camurri, A., Volpe, G., Piana, S., Mancini, M., Niewiadomski, R., Ferrari, N., Canepa, C.: The dancer in the eye: towards a multi-layered computational framework of qualities in movement. In: 3rd International Symposium on Movement and Computing, MOCO 2016 (2016)
6. Dempster, W.T., Gaughran, G.R.L.: Properties of body segments based on size and weight. Am. J. Anat. **120**(1), 33–54 (1967). http://dx.doi.org/10.1002/aja.1001200104
7. Folke, M., Cernerud, L., Ekström, M., Hök, B.: Critical review of non-invasive respiratory monitoring in medical care. Med. Biol. Eng. Comput. **41**(4), 377–383 (2003)
8. Hoffmann, C.P., Torregrosa, G., Bardy, B.G.: Sound stabilizes locomotor-respiratory coupling and reduces energy cost. PLoS ONE **7**(9), e45206 (2012)
9. Huq, S., Yadollahi, A., Moussavi, Z.: Breath analysis of respiratory flow using tracheal sounds. In: 2007 IEEE International Symposium on Signal Processing and Information Technology, pp. 414–418 (2007)
10. Jin, F., Sattar, F., Goh, D., Louis, I.M.: An enhanced respiratory rate monitoring method for real tracheal sound recordings. In: 2009 17th European Signal Processing Conference, pp. 642–645 (2009)
11. Kim, J., Andre, E.: Emotion recognition based on physiological changes in music listening. IEEE Trans. Pattern Anal. Mach. Intell. **30**(12), 2067–2083 (2008)
12. Laban, R., Lawrence, F.C.: Effort. Macdonald & Evans, London (1947)
13. Liu, G., Guo, Y., Zhu, Q., Huang, B., Wang, L.: Estimation of respiration rate from three-dimensional acceleration data based on body sensor network. Telemed. J. e-Health **17**(9), 705–711 (2011)
14. Niewiadomski, R., Mancini, M., Piana, S.: Human and virtual agent expressive gesture quality analysis and synthesis. In: Rojc, M., Campbell, N. (eds.) Coverbal Synchrony in Human-Machine Interaction, pp. 269–292. CRC Press (2013)
15. Niewiadomski, R., Mancini, M., Ding, Y., Pelachaud, C., Volpe, G.: Rhythmic body movements of laughter. In: Proceedings of the 16th International Conference on Multimodal Interaction. ICMI 2014, New York, pp. 299–306 (2014). http://doi.acm.org/10.1145/2663204.2663240
16. Niewiadomski, R., Mancini, M., Volpe, G., Camurri, A.: Automated detection of impulsive movements in HCI. In: Proceedings of the 11th Biannual Conference on Italian SIGCHI Chapter, CHItaly 2015, New York, pp. 166–169 (2015). http://doi.acm.org/10.1145/2808435.2808466
17. Piana, S., Coletta, P., Ghisio, S., Niewiadomski, R., Mancini, M., Sagoleo, R., Volpe, G., Camurri, A.: Towards a multimodal repository of expressive movement qualities in dance. In: 3rd International Symposium on Movement and Computing, MOCO 2016 (2016). http://dx.doi.org/10.1145/2948910.2948931
18. Piana, S., Alborno, P., Niewiadomski, R., Mancini, M., Volpe, G., Camurri, A.: Movement fluidity analysis based on performance and perception. In: Proceedings of the 2016 CHI Conference Extended Abstracts on Human Factors in Computing Systems, CHI EA 2016, New York, pp. 1629–1636 (2016). http://doi.acm.org/10.1145/2851581.2892478

19. Quian Quiroga, R., Kreuz, T., Grassberger, P.: Event synchronization: a simple and fast method to measure synchronicity and time delay patterns. Phys. Rev. E **66**, 041904. http://link.aps.org/doi/10.1103/PhysRevE.66.041904
20. Rao, K.M., Sudarshan, B.: A review on different technical specifications of respiratory rate monitors. IJRET: Int. J. Res. Eng. Technol. **4**(4), 424–429 (2015)
21. Ruinskiy, D., Lavner, Y.: An effective algorithm for automatic detection and exact demarcation of breath sounds in speech and song signals. IEEE Trans. Audio Speech Lang. Process. **15**(3), 838–850 (2007)
22. Schmid, M., Conforto, S., Bibbo, D., D'Alessio, T.: Respiration and postural sway: detection of phase synchronizations and interactions. Hum. Mov. Sci. **23**(2), 105–119 (2004)
23. Yahya, O., Faezipour, M.: Automatic detection and classification of acoustic breathing cycles. In: 2014 Zone 1 Conference of the American Society for Engineering Education (ASEE Zone 1), pp. 1–5, April 2014

Spatio-Temporal Detection of Fine-Grained Dyadic Human Interactions

Coert van Gemeren[✉], Ronald Poppe, and Remco C. Veltkamp

Interaction Technology Group, Department of Information and Computing Sciences,
Utrecht University, Utrecht, The Netherlands
{C.J.VanGemeren,R.W.Poppe,R.C.Veltkamp}@uu.nl

Abstract. We introduce a novel spatio-temporal deformable part model for offline detection of fine-grained interactions in video. One novelty of the model is that part detectors model the interacting individuals in a single graph that can contain different combinations of feature descriptors. This allows us to use both body pose and movement to model the coordination between two people in space and time. We evaluate the performance of our approach on novel and existing interaction datasets. When testing only on the target class, we achieve mean average precision scores of 0.82. When presented with distractor classes, the additional modelling of the motion of specific body parts significantly reduces the number of confusions. Cross-dataset tests demonstrate that our trained models generalize well to other settings.

Keywords: Human behavior · Interaction detection · Spatio-temporal localization

1 Introduction

Action recognition in videos continues to attract a significant amount of research attention [14]. Starting from the analysis of individuals performing particular actions in isolation (e.g. [19]), there is a trend towards the contextual analysis of people in action. There is much interest in the understanding of a person's actions and interactions in a social context, with research into the automated recognition of group actions [2] and human-human interactions [13,17].

This paper contributes to the latter category. We focus on two-person (*dyadic*) interactions such as shaking hands, passing objects or hugging. The type of interaction in which people engage informs us of their activity, the social and cultural setting and the relation between them. Automated detection of interactions can improve social surveillance, for example to differentiate between friendly and hostile interactions or to determine whether a person in an elderly home is a staff member, family member or unrelated visitor.

Poses of people in different interactions can be visually similar, for example when shaking hands or handing over an object (see Fig. 1). To differentiate

---

This publication was supported by the Dutch national program COMMIT.

M. Chetouani et al. (Eds.): HBU 2016, LNCS 9997, pp. 116–133, 2016.
DOI: 10.1007/978-3-319-46843-3_8

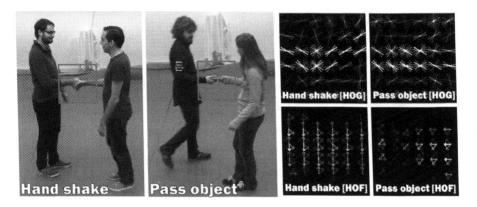

Fig. 1. Hand shake and object pass interactions with similar poses. We introduce a model to detect interactions that differ slightly in their spatio-temporal coordination by modeling pose and motion of specific body parts.

between interactions, the *coordinated movement* of the people provides an additional cue. Not all body parts play an equally important role in each interaction. For example, a hand shake is characterized by the movement of the right hands. The distinction between such interactions requires a *fine-grained* analysis of the specific pose and body motion of both persons involved in the interaction.

In this paper, we detect dyadic interactions based on structural models [29] that combine pose (HOG) and movement (HOF) information. We train classifiers from videos and focus on those parts of the video that characterize the interaction. This enables us to distinguish between interactions that differ only slightly. An advantage of our method is that we can detect where the interaction occurs in a video in both space and time. This property allows us to identify who is involved in the interaction, or who hands over an object to whom.

Our *contributions* are as follows. First, we model the coordinated body movement of the people involved. We introduce a novel model to exploit these cues and to detect interactions in both space and time. Second, we present a procedure to train a detector from a few examples with pose information. Third, we demonstrate the performance of our framework on publicly available datasets. We report spatio-temporal localization performance for models trained only on the target interaction class.

We discuss related work in the next section. In Sect. 3, we introduce our model and detail the training and test procedures. The evaluation of our work appears in Sect. 4. We conclude in Sect. 5.

2   Related Work on Interaction Detection

The progress of vision-based action recognition algorithms is impressive [14]. Initial success was mainly based on bag-of-visual-word (BoVW) approaches that map image feature distributions to action labels [19]. Wang et al. [26] link these features over time into dense trajectories, allowing for more robust representations of movement. The work has been extended by clustering the trajectories to enable the *spatio-temporal* detection of actions [25].

While these representations have achieved state-of-the-art performance, they do not explicitly link image features to human body parts. The availability of body pose and, especially, body movement information has been found to increase action classification performance [5]. This is because the pose or movement of some body parts is often characteristic. For example, arm movement is more discriminative than leg movement in a hand shake. Without pose information, discriminative patterns of image movement can only be modeled implicitly, e.g. using clusters of dense trajectories [11] or co-occurring spatio-temporal words [32]. These approaches are automatic but less reliable in the presence of other motions, when multiple people interact with each other in close proximity.

Part-based models such as Deformable Part Models (DPM, [3]) and poselets [1] can detect people in an image and localize their body parts. These models employ body part detectors and impose spatial constraints between these parts. DPMs are sufficiently flexible to describe articulations of the body [29]. This enables the detection of key poses representative of an action [15]. Often, two actions cannot be distinguished based on a single key pose, see Fig. 1. Movement can then be used to distinguish between classes [23]. Yao et al. [30] represent actions as a combination of a pose and a mixture of motion templates.

In this paper, we follow this line of research, but extend it to the detection of interactions. Researchers have started to analyze behavior of multiple people [2,9]. Here, we focus on the recognition of two-person interactions. Recent work in this area has used gross body movement and proximity cues for the detection of interactions. A common approach is to first detect faces or bodies using off-the-shelf detectors [13,18]. Detections of individuals can be paired and the resulting bounding volume can be used to pool features in a BoVW approach [10].

The relative distances and orientations between people can also be used to characterize interactions. Patron-Perez et al. [13] use coarse distance labels (e.g., far, overlap) and differences in head orientation. They also include local features around each person such as histograms of oriented gradients (HOG) and flow (HOF). Sener and İkizler [21] take a similar approach but cast the training as multiple-instance learning, as not all frames in an interaction are considered informative. For the same reason, Sefidgar et al. [20] extract discriminative key frames and consider their relative distance and timing within the interaction.

Kong and Fu [7] observe that not all body parts contribute equally. Their method pools BoVW responses in a coarse grid. This allows them to identify specific motion patterns relative to a person's location but the level of detail of the analysis is limited by the granularity of the patches and the accuracy of the person detector. Yang et al. [28] found that a sequential approach of first detecting individuals and then recognizing their interaction does not perform well when there is physical contact. They significantly improve classification performance by building detectors for various types of physical interactions such as hand-hand and hand-shoulder touches. Here we also focus on physical interactions, but we look at the *fine-grained* differences between visually similar classes.

Proximity and orientation are good cues for detection of coarse interaction classes, but less so to detect fine-grained interactions such as those in social encounters. These are characterized by body movements that are visually similar, but differ slightly in the temporal coordination. To distinguish between such interactions, we need to more effectively model the coordination between the people involved.

Kong et al. [8] train detectors for attributes such as "outstretched hands" and "leaning forward torso" and consider their co-occurrences. Given sufficiently detailed attributes, fine-grained interactions could be detected. However, as each detector is applied independently, false detections are likely to occur. van Gemeren et al. [24] use interaction-specific DPMs to locate people in characteristic poses. They then describe the coordinated movement in the region in between DPM detections. As there can be significant variation in how people pose, this two-stage approach strongly relies on the accuracy of the pose detection.

In this paper, we address this issue by combining the detection of the people and their interaction in a single step. We diverge from Yao et al. [30], by constraining how pose and motion are coordinated in a dyadic scenario, so we can model spatio-temporal coordination at a much more fine-grained level. Yao et al. train and test their model on human-object interaction tasks, whereas we focus specifically on dyadic human interactions.

3   Modeling Fine-Grained Coordinated Interactions

We model two-person interactions based on DPMs for pose recognition in images, introduced by Yang and Ramanan [29]. We solve three limitations. First, parts are not locally centered on body joints but are specific for an interaction and typically encode the relative position and articulation of a body part, similar to poselets [1]. Second, we allow each part detector to contain multiple image cues. We explicitly enable the combination of static and temporal features. We can thus decide per body part whether pose, motion or a combination is most discriminative for a specific interaction. Third, we consider two persons simultaneously. Our formulation models the spatial and temporal coordination between their poses and movements at a fine scale. We discuss the model, training algorithm and detection procedure subsequently.

3.1   Model Formulation

Our model is motivated by the observation that many interactions are characterized by a moment where the poses of two people are spatially coordinated and the movement of a specific part of the body is temporally coordinated.

Let us define graph $G = (V, E)$, with V a set of K body parts and E the set of connections between pairs of parts [29]. Each body part i is centered on location $l_i = (x_i, y_i)$. For clarity, we omit in our formulation the extent of the body part's area, as well as scaling due to processing an image i at multiple resolutions. The scoring for a part configuration in image I is given by:

$$S(I, l) = \sum_{i \in P} w_i \cdot \phi_i(I, l_i) + \sum_{ij \in E} w_{ij} \cdot \psi(l_i - l_j) \qquad (1)$$

The first term models the part appearance with a convolution of image feature vector $\phi_i(I, l_i)$ with trained detector w_i. The second term contains the pair-wise deformations between parts $\psi(l_i - l_j) = [dx \; dx^2 \; dy \; dy^2]$, with $dx = r_i x_i - r_j x_j$ and $dy = r_i y_i - r_j y_j$ the relative location of part i with respect to part j [29]. These distances are defined with respect to root factor r, which allows for scaling of parts with a different cell resolution as the root part [3]. w_{ij} encodes the rest location and the rigidity of the connections between parts.

We now describe our adaptations of this model for the modeling of fine-grained dyadic interactions.

Class-specific Part Detectors. While [29] considers different body part orientations as parameters in the model, we learn class-specific detectors that encode the articulation of the body part directly. Though our method allows for modeling multiple mixtures per part, our data only features homogeneous interactions recorded from a specific viewing angle. Therefore, we use only a single detector per class, instead of a mixture of part detectors. Aside from having data that features interactions performed in different ways from multiple viewpoints, increasing the amount of mixtures would also require a larger amount of samples.

Multiple Features. Our model supports different types of features per part. For part i with feature representations D_i, we replace the first term in Eq. 1 by:

$$\sum_{i \in P} \sum_{j \in D_i} b_{ij} w_i^j \cdot \phi_i^j(I, l_i) \qquad (2)$$

$\phi_i^j(I, l_i)$ denotes a feature vector of type j (e.g., HOG or HOF) for part i. Bias b_{ij} denotes the weight for each feature type. w_i^j is the trained detector for part i and feature type j. Parts can have different combinations of features D_i. As such, our formulation is different from Yao et al. [30], who require one HOG template and a set of HOF templates per body part. In contrast, our model allows us to focus on those features that are characteristic for a specific body part and interaction class. We explicitly also consider features that are calculated over time such as HOF descriptors.

Two-person Interaction. As there are two persons involved in a dyadic interaction, we combine their body parts into the same graph. Each actor's body parts form a sub-tree in this $(2K + 1)$-node graph. The torso parts of both actors are connected through a virtual root part of the graph. This part does not have an associated part detector but it allows us to model relative distances between people. To our knowledge currently no methods exist that model dyadic interactions as a single part based model.

In the experiments presented in this paper, the sub-tree of each person has a *torso* root node with four child parts: *head*, *right upper arm*, *right lower arm* and *right hand*.

3.2   Training

For each interaction class, we learn the model from a set of training sequences. We describe a sequence of length n as $X = \{(I_i, y_i, p_i)\}_{i=1}^{n}$ with I_i an image frame, y_i the interaction label of frame i and p_i a pose vector containing the 2D joint positions of the two persons performing the dyadic interaction. The metadata of the training videos contains 3D skeleton joint positions, from which we calculate 2D projections. We use this to place parts on limb locations. We assume the sequences are segmented in time to contain the interaction of interest. As the temporal segmentation relies on human annotations the start and the end of an interaction are not precisely marked. Therefore we consider a single short sequence of frames most representative for the interaction in each sequence, as the base of the model. We call this sequence the *epitome*. We guarantee that the epitome is taken from the temporally segmented sequence.

Fig. 2. Frame with superimposed pose data. (Color figure online)

Training consists of three steps. First, we determine the epitome frame per training sequence. Second, we learn the initial body part detectors. Third, we simultaneously update the epitome frame and the body part detectors.

Epitome Frame Detection. We intend to find the prototypical interaction frame of each training sequence. To this end, we pair-wise compare the joint sets of all frames in two sequences. For our experiments, we consider all joints in the right arm of both persons in interaction (green parts in Fig. 2). We can efficiently identify the epitome in each sequence with the Kabsch algorithm [6]. We use it to compare sets of coordinates in a translation, scale and rotationally invariant way. Based on the Kabsch distance between the video with the lowest sum distance to all other videos, we label each sequence as *prime* if this distance is below 0.5, and *inferior* otherwise. Essentially we separate the videos in which the skeleton poses look-alike, from the videos where they don't.

Initial Model Learning. We learn body part detectors w_i^j (Eq. 2) from the prime sequences. We determine, for each part, the type, spatial resolution and temporal extent. In this paper, we consider HOG and HOF features [26] but the DPM inference algorithm is well suited to incorporate a learned feature extractor such as convolutional neural networks (CNN) [4]. The spatial resolution indicates the cell size. For HOF, the temporal extent dictates how many frames around the epitome frame are used.

For each interaction, we train body part detectors for both persons using Dual Coordinate Descent SVM (DCD SVM) solvers [22]. After the positive optimization round, we perform a round of hard negative detection [3]. Negative examples are harvested in random frames of the Hannah dataset [12], to avoid overfitting

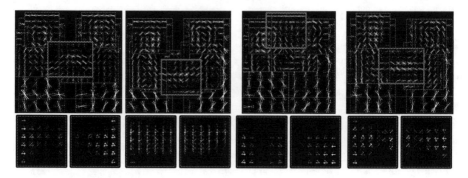

Fig. 3. Top row: HOG pose models for fist bump, hand shake, high five and pass object. Bottom row: HOF features of the right hands. The red rectangle indicates the enclosing bounding box of the two hands. (Color figure online)

to a particular training set, and to allow for the extraction of realistic motion patches. After optimizing all part mixtures, we combine all parts into a single spatio-temporal DPM (SDPM). The locations of the parts are based on the average relative center locations in the pose data.

Epitome and Model Refinement. Once an initial SDPM is constructed, we apply it to both prime and inferior training sequences to detect new latent positive interaction examples. We search for the highest scoring frame in each sequence to update the positive example set. Given that the initial epitome frames are selected solely based on pose, this step allows us to better represent the motion of the body. The resulting positive example set is used to optimize the model features and to determine all part biases and deformation parameters using the DCD SVM solvers. Example models are shown in Fig. 3. Note the vertical hand movement for the hand shake model and the horizontal movement for fist bump.

3.3   Spatio-Temporal Localization

With a trained SDPM, we can detect interactions in both space and time. We specifically avoid 3D feature extraction during training because we want to be able to apply our model on data that does not contain any depth information. We first detect interactions in frame sequences that last shorter than a second, and then link these to form interaction tubes, without the use of depth information.

We generate a feature pyramid for each of the feature types to detect interactions at various scales. We extend the formulation to deal with feature types with a temporal extent. Based on Eq. 1, we generate a set of detection candidates spanning the entire video. In practice, we evaluate non-overlapping video segments. For a temporal HOF size of nine frames, we evaluate every ninth frame. Overlapping detections are removed with non-maximum suppression.

Interaction Tubes. We link frame detections into interaction tubes (see Fig. 4). We sort candidate detections on detection score. Each tube starts with the best scoring detection. We then greedily assign the detections of adjacent frames to the current tube. A detection is only added if it satisfies a minimum spatial overlap constraint ρ of 50 % and a maximum area deviation of 50 % with respect to the best detection. We iterate until all candidate detections have been assigned to a tube. Finally we remove all tubes with only a single detection.

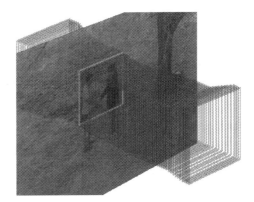

Fig. 4. Detected spatio-temporal interaction tube (red) for a hand shake. The green rectangle shows the best detection. (Color figure online)

4   Experiments and Results

Previous research on interaction *recognition* has considered assigning labels to video sequences that have been segmented in both space and time. In contrast, we focus on *spatio-temporal detection* of interactions from unsegmented videos. To address this scenario, we present a novel dataset and our performance measures. Subsequently, we summarize the setup and results of our experiments.

4.1   Datasets

As available interaction datasets contain behaviors that are visually quite dissimilar, we introduce a novel dataset *ShakeFive2*[1] with interactions that differ slightly in their coordination. We train interaction detection models on this dataset and present the performance of different settings. In addition, we test these models on publicly available interaction datasets *SBU Kinect* [31] and *UT-Interaction* [17]. Example frames from each of these datasets can be seen in Fig. 5.

ShakeFive2 consists of 94 videos with five close proximity interaction classes: *fist bump*, *hand shake*, *high five*, *hug* and *pass object*. Each video contains one two-person interaction, recorded under controlled settings but with small variations in viewpoint. We note that in the pass object interaction a small orange object is passed from one person to the other. This is the same small object for all videos. For each person in each frame, 3D joint position data obtained using Kinect2 is available.

---

[1] *ShakeFive2* is publicly available from https://goo.gl/ObHv36.

Fig. 5. Example frames from the datasets used in this paper: ShakeFive2, SBU Kinect and UT-Interaction. Top row: hand shake, bottom row: hug.

SBU Kinect involves two actors performing one interaction per video in an indoors setting. The interactions are: *hand shake, high five, hug, pass object, kick, leave, punch* and *push*. Pose data, obtained with a Kinect, is provided but not always accurate. From the 260 videos, we exclude 42 with incorrect pose data.

UT-Interaction consists of two sets of 10 videos each. The first set features two persons in interaction per video, while the second set contains multiple pairs per video. The following interactions are performed: *hand shake, hug, kick, point, punch* and *push*. No pose data is available but bounding boxes are provided. These span the entire spatial extent of the interaction. To have a more tight estimate of the interaction per frame, we use the bounding box data from [21].

4.2   Performance Measurements

As we detect interactions in both space and time, we use the average intersection over union of the ground truth G and detected tube P as in [25]. G and P are two sets of bounding boxes and θ is the set of frames in which either P or G is not empty. The overlap is calculated as:

$$IoU(G, P) = \frac{1}{\|\theta\|} \sum_{f \in \theta} \frac{G_f \cap P_f}{G_f \cup P_f} \tag{3}$$

We evaluate different minimal overlap thresholds σ for which $IoU(G, P) \geq \sigma$. For cross-validation tests, we create one precision-recall diagram per fold. We report the mean average precision (mAP) scores as the mean of the areas under the curves of each fold.

We consider two testing scenarios: single-class (SC) and multi-class (MC). For *single-class* detection, we apply a detector for a given interaction class to test videos of that class only. This scenario measures the spatio-temporal localization accuracy. In the *multi-class* scenario, we test the detector on all available test sequences in the dataset. This allows us to determine whether there are confusions with other interactions. In the multi-class scenario, the same interaction can be detected with models of different classes. This common situation will lead to false positives as we do not compare or filter these detections. The reported mAP scores are therefore conservative but demonstrate the performance of our models without discriminative training.

To assess which pairs of classes are more often confused, we introduce a novel measure that takes into account the spatio-temporal nature of our problem. We test a trained detector in the single-class and multi-class detection scenarios and calculate the difference in mAP (d-mAP) scores between these two settings. When no false positives have been identified, the d-mAP score is zero. Higher d-mAP scores are due to the performance loss caused by the false positives for the particular distractor class.

4.3 Features and Experiment Setup

Our model can be trained using different types of descriptors per part. In our experiments, we consider HOG and HOF descriptors. For HOG, we use the gradient description method of [3], which differs slightly from [26]. Optical flow is calculated with DeepFlow [27]. For the time dimension of HOF, we use three bins of three frames each. For a 30 fps video, this covers about a third of a second.

We use a **HOG** model that describes the torso with 4×8 cells, the right upper arm with 7×8, right lower arm with 9×7 and the right hand and head with 6×6 cells. The number of pixels per cell is 8×8 for the torso and 4×4 for other body parts. The **HOF** model is similar but all body parts are encoded as HOF. The **HOGHOF** model describes the torso and head as HOG, the right upper and lower arms as HOG and HOF and the right hand with HOF.

Models are trained on the data of ShakeFive2 using three-fold cross-validation. In each fold, there are six or seven sequences per class. We therefore train on either 12 or 13 sequences only. The performance in the single-class scenario is calculated as the average performance over the three folds. In the multi-class scenario, we combine the test folds of the different interaction classes, creating a set of 30–34 videos of which six or seven are of the target class.

4.4 Detection Results

We first investigate the added value of using motion information for interaction detection. We test the **HOG**, **HOF** and **HOGHOF** models on the ShakeFive2 dataset. We refer to the five interactions as FB (fist bump), HS (hand shake), HF (high five), HU (hug) and PO (pass object). Results for the single-class (SC) and multi-class (MC) scenarios are shown in Table 1. We use a minimal overlap σ between the detected tube and the ground truth volume (Eq. 3) of 10 %.

When tested on only videos of the same class (SC), we see that the **HOGHOF** model outperforms both **HOG** and **HOF**. This demonstrates that interactions are most accurately detected by a combination of pose and motion information.

Table 1. Single-class (SC) and multi-class (MC) mAP scores on ShakeFive2.

	SC/MC	FB	HS	HF	HU	PO	Avg.
HOG	SC	0.74	0.79	0.75	0.61	0.95	**0.77**
HOF	SC	0.55	0.75	0.70	0.65	0.55	**0.64**
HOGHOF	SC	0.83	0.95	0.83	0.61	0.88	**0.82**
HOG	MC	0.32	0.55	0.39	0.37	0.63	**0.45**
HOF	MC	0.23	0.60	0.48	0.51	0.28	**0.42**
HOGHOF	MC	0.54	0.88	0.50	0.34	0.57	**0.57**

The lower performance of **HOF** indicates that movement information alone is not sufficient to robustly detect interactions from video. When additional sequences of other interaction classes are available (MC), we notice a significant drop for all models but less so for **HOGHOF**. Especially the lack of pose information in the **HOF** model appears to cause misclassifications between interactions. The combination of pose and motion in the **HOGHOF** model appears to work best. Note that all models are trained on at most 13 positive training sequences and that the other interactions are not provided as negative samples. The models are therefore not trained to discriminate between interaction classes.

Table 2. d-mAP scores for the **HOG** (left) and **HOGHOF** (right) models on Shake-Five2. In columns the true class, in rows the tested class.

	FB	HS	HF	HU	PO
FB		0.41	0.24	0.16	0.44
HS	0.22		0.15	0.15	0.31
HF	0.32	0.31		0.20	0.25
HU	0.23	0.26	0.23		0.19
PO	0.15	0.27	0.07	0.05	

	FB	HS	HF	HU	PO
FB		0.19	0.16	0.13	0.28
HS	0.04		0.04	0.04	0.09
HF	0.26	0.19		0.11	0.16
HU	0.29	0.18	0.24		0.22
PO	0.19	0.25	0.09	0.05	

There are some differences in performance between the interaction classes. Hand shakes can be detected relatively robustly by all models, whereas especially hugs are often not detected. In the multi-class setting, we can investigate how often interaction classes are confused. We present the d-mAP multi-class detection scores on ShakeFive2 for the **HOG** and **HOGHOF** models in Table 2. For the **HOG** model, there are many confusions. Apparently, the pose information alone is not sufficiently informative to distinguish between interactions that differ slightly in temporal coordination: hand shake, fist bump and pass object. The number of confusions for the **HOGHOF** model is much lower. The additional motion information can be used to reduce the number of misclassification between visually similar interactions.

We note that especially fist bump and hand shake have fewer confusions with the **HOGHOF** model compared to the **HOG** model. However, the **HOGHOF** model for pass object has more confusions. We expect that the variation in the performance of this interaction leads to a suboptimal model during training. This can be seen in Fig. 3 as well. The HOG description of the pose is somewhat ambiguous, while the HOF descriptor of the hands is similar for the pass object and fist bump interactions. Indeed, many pass object interactions are detected as fist bumps.

4.5   Parameter Settings

Next, we investigate the influence on the detection performance of the most important parameters of our models: the minimal tube overlap (σ), the minimal spatial overlap (ρ) and the number of training sequences.

Minimal tube overlap is a measure of how accurate the detections are in both space and time. A higher threshold σ requires more accurate detection. In line with [25], we vary this threshold from 0.1 to 0.5. Figure 6 shows the performance of the three models for increasing σ. We note that **HOG** (Fig. 6a) shows a better performance than **HOF** (Fig. 6b) when σ increases. When HOG and HOF are combined (**HOGHOF**, in Fig. 6c), we observe a significant increase in performance and mAP scores that remain higher for larger values of σ.

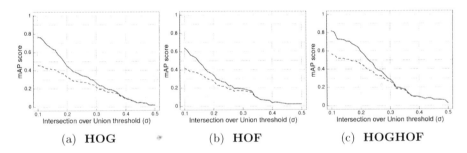

(a) **HOG**   (b) **HOF**   (c) **HOGHOF**

Fig. 6. mAP scores over all interaction classes in the single-class (solid line) and multi-class (dashed) scenarios of ShakeFive2 for increasing values of σ.

Minimal Spatial Overlap. Subsequent detections in time are linked provided that they sufficiently overlap spatially. The default threshold ρ of 50 % is in line with object detection research but Fig. 7a shows the mAP scores for different values of ρ, with best results for $\rho = 58\%$. A higher value for ρ results in fewer links and, consequently, smaller tubes. With a lower threshold, noisy detections are more often linked to the tube, also resulting in a lower mAP.

Amount of Training Data. We noticed that the **HOGHOF** models achieve good detection performance despite being trained on a small number of example sequences. Here we test the performance of the model when

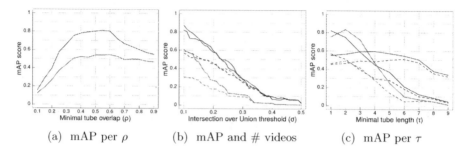

(a) mAP per ρ (b) mAP and # videos   (c) mAP per τ

Fig. 7. mAP scores for different parameter settings in the single-class (solid line) and multi-class (dashed) scenarios. (a) shows the influence of the minimal spatial overlap on the performance. (b) shows the performance with different amounts of training videos: 2 (red), 12–13 (blue) or 15–16 (green). (c) shows the influence on the minimal tube overlap for different datasets: ShakeFive2 (blue), SBU Kinect (red) and UT-Interaction (green). (Color figure online)

trained on different numbers of sequences. Figure 7b shows the mAP scores when training on 2, 12–13 (3 folds), and 15–16 (6 folds) sequences. For the first setting, we sampled pairs of training sequences. Clearly, performance is lower when training on just two training sequences. The difference between 12–13 and 15–16 sequences is very small. This suggests that saturation occurs at a very low number of training data. This is advantageous as obtaining training sequences with associated pose data might be difficult, especially when many interaction classes are considered.

4.6   Performance on SBU Kinect and UT-Interaction

To compare our method to previous work, we also evaluate the performance on publicly available interaction datasets SBU Kinect and UT-Interaction. We train **HOGHOF** models on all available sequences in ShakeFive2. Results reported are for *cross-dataset* evaluation. In the single-class scenario, we only report the interactions are shared between ShakeFive2 and the other two datasets. We evaluate all available videos in the dataset in the multi-class scenario.

Even though the three datasets are similar in the type of interaction, there are several notable differences. First, there is variation between the datasets in the viewpoint and the performance of the interactions (see also Fig. 5). For example, the average durations of hand shakes in ShakeFive2 and UT-Interaction are 27 and 100 frames, respectively, both at 30 frames per second. Also, the percentage of positive interaction frames differs. For UT-Interaction, 5 % of the frames contain the interaction of interest. This is 12 % for ShakeFive2, and all frames of SBU Interact contain the target interaction.

To account for differences in interaction length, we introduce minimal tube length τ. Tubes shorter than τ segments are removed. This is beneficial for datasets with significantly longer interactions than in the training data. Figure 7c summarizes the performance of the **HOGHOF** model on the evaluated datasets.

Table 3. Single-class (SC) and multi-class (MC) mAP scores for SBU Kinect.

	SC/MC	HS	HU	PO
HOGHOF	SC	0.94	0.68	0.87
HOGHOF	MC	0.71	0.53	0.24

ShakeFive2 and SBU Kinect have similar profiles, UT-Interaction scores better for τ values around 4. For SBU Kinect and UT-Interaction, we set $\tau = 2$.

SBU Kinect. Table 3 summarizes the performance on SBU Kinect. We have tested the "noisy" variation of this dataset using our **HOGHOF** model with $\sigma = 0.1$, $\rho = 0.5$ and $\tau = 2$. We observe high scores in the single-class scenario, even though we did not train on this dataset. For comparison, Yun et al. [31] report classification performance on the dataset when using the pose features. They obtain 75 %, 61 % and 85 % recognition accuracy for the hand shake, hug and pass object interactions, respectively. While these scores cannot be compared directly, it is clear that classification of segmented sequences already presents challenges. Detecting the interaction in space and time adds to the challenge.

Table 4. d-mAP scores for the **HOGHOF** models on SBU Kinect. In columns the true class, in rows the tested class.

	HS	HU	KI	LV	PC	PS	PO
HS		0.03	0.08	0.06	0.12	0.18	0.14
HU	0.18		0.21	0.14	0.22	0.24	0.26
PO	0.38	0.08	0.22	0.29	0.23	0.40	

We note that the detection of the pass object interaction scores particularly low in the multi-class setting compared to the single-class setting. To analyze confusions, Table 4 presents d-mAP values for all SBU Kinect interactions: hand shake (HS), hug (HU), kick (KI), leave (LV), punch (PC), push (PS) and pass object (PO). Many hand shake and push interactions are detected as pass object. These three interactions are characterized by extended, horizontally moving arms. The pass object model clearly is not discriminative enough to pick up on the subtle differences between the interactions.

UT-Interaction. Finally, we evaluate the **HOGHOF** models on the UT-Interaction dataset. Results of our model and previously reported results are summarized in Table 5. A direct comparison with other works is difficult for a number of reasons. First, we report detection results only for hand shake and hug, the common interactions between ShakeFive2 and UT-Interaction. Second, we report spatio-temporal localization results, whereas other works consider a recognition scenario. In this setting, volumes segmented in space and time are classified. Third, we train our models on a different dataset.

Table 5. Single-class (SC) and multi-class (MC) mAP scores for UT-Interaction (left). Classification accuracies reported on UT-Interaction (right).

(left)

	Set	HS	HU	Avg.
SC	#1	0.61	0.39	**0.57**
	#2	0.90	0.36	
MC	#1	0.48	0.38	**0.46**
	#2	0.63	0.36	

(right)

Method	Avg.
Raptis and Sigal [15]	100 %
Ryoo [16]	85 %
Sener and İkizler [21]	100 %
Zhang et al. [32]	100 %

Table 5 shows the detection results on both sets of UT-Interaction. Our **HOGHOF** can detect multiple simultaneous interaction, as witnessed by the scores on set 2. The detection of hugs is much lower. We attribute this to the longer duration of the hugs. Many hugs are not detected for a sufficient number of subsequent frames. As a result, there are missed detections. Higher values for τ can alleviate this problem.

5   Conclusions and Future Work

We have introduced a novel model for the detection of two-person interactions. Our spatio-temporal deformable part models combine pose and motion in such a way that we can model the fine-grained coordination of specific body parts. For the first time, we address the spatio-temporal detection of interactions from unsegmented video. Our approach allows us not only to say whether an interaction has occurred, but also to recover its spatial and temporal extent.

Interaction models are trained from only a few videos with pose information. On the novel ShakeFive2 dataset, we achieve mAP scores of 0.82 when training on 12–13 sequences. In the presence of visually similar interactions, motion information reduces the number of misclassifications. We obtain mAP scores of 0.57 without discriminative training, and without filtering the detections. Moreover, our cross-dataset evaluations on the publicly available UT-Interaction and SBU Kinect datasets demonstrate that the model generalizes to different settings.

Despite its good performance, the method has some limitations. Most importantly, the number of false detections is considerable. Currently, we can have several detections of the same interaction. By filtering these, we can reduce the number of false positives. This will allow us to report classification results. Another improvement is the discriminative training of the interaction models.

This is likely to improve the detection performance as each model can focus on those parts of the pose or motion that are discriminative for the interaction.

Pose data is required to train our models. We are considering incremental training schemes that alleviate this need. Finally, we would like to include multiple perspectives to improve viewpoint independence. While there is some variation within and between the datasets that we have evaluated, viewpoint invariance will further increase the applicability of our work.

Together, we envision that these improvements can bring closer the automated spatio-temporal detection of a broad range of social interactions in unconstrained video material. This will allow for the automated analysis of TV footage and web videos. Moreover, we aim at the application of our work in dedicated social surveillance settings such as in public meeting places and elderly homes.

References

1. Bourdev, L., Maji, S., Brox, T., Malik, J.: Detecting people using mutually consistent poselet activations. In: Daniilidis, K., Maragos, P., Paragios, N. (eds.) ECCV 2010. LNCS, vol. 6316, pp. 168–181. Springer, Heidelberg (2010). doi:10.1007/978-3-642-15567-3_13
2. Choi, W., Savarese, S.: Understanding collective activities of people from videos. IEEE Trans. Pattern Anal. Mach. Intell. (PAMI) **36**(6), 1242–1257 (2014)
3. Felzenszwalb, P.F., Girshick, R.B., McAllester, D.A., Ramanan, D.: Object detection with discriminatively trained part-based models. IEEE Trans. Pattern Anal. Mach. Intell. (PAMI) **32**(9), 1627–1645 (2010)
4. Girshick, R., Iandola, F., Darrell, T., Malik, J.: Deformable part models are convolutional neural networks. In: Proceedings Conference on Computer Vision and Pattern Recognition (CVPR), pp. 437–446 (2015)
5. Jhuang, H., Gall, J., Zuffi, S., Schmid, C., Black, M.J.: Towards understanding action recognition. In: Proceedings IEEE International Conference on Computer Vision (ICCV), pp. 3192–3199 (2013)
6. Kabsch, W.: A discussion of the solution for the best rotation to relate two sets of vectors. Acta Crystallogr. Sect. A **34**(5), 827–828 (1978)
7. Kong, Y., Fu, Y.: Close human interaction recognition using patch-aware models. IEEE Trans. Image Process. (TIP) **25**(1), 167–178 (2015)
8. Kong, Y., Jia, Y., Fu, Y.: Interactive phrases: semantic descriptions for human interaction recognition. IEEE Trans. Pattern Anal. Mach. Intell. (PAMI) **36**(9), 1775–1788 (2014)
9. Lan, T., Wang, Y., Yang, W., Robinovitch, S.N., Mori, G.: Discriminative latent models for recognizing contextual group activities. IEEE Trans. Pattern Anal. Mach. Intell. (PAMI) **34**(8), 1549–1562 (2012)
10. Marín-Jiménez, M.J., Yeguas, E., Pérez de la Blanca, N.: Exploring STIP-based models for recognizing human interactions in TV videos. Pattern Recognit. Lett. **34**(15), 1819–1828 (2013)
11. Ni, B., Moulin, P., Yang, X., Yan, S.: Motion part regularization: improving action recognition via trajectory selection. In: Proceedings Conference on Computer Vision and Pattern Recognition (CVPR), pp. 3698–3706 (2015)
12. Ozerov, A., Vigouroux, J., Chevallier, L., Pérez, P.: On evaluating face tracks in movies. In: Proceedings International Conference on Image Processing (ICIP), pp. 3003–3007 (2013)

13. Patron-Perez, A., Marszałek, M., Reid, I., Zisserman, A.: Structured learning of human interactions in TV shows. IEEE Trans. Pattern Anal. Mach. Intell. (PAMI) **34**(12), 2441–2453 (2012)
14. Poppe, R.: A survey on vision-based human action recognition. Image Vis. Comput. **28**(6), 976–990 (2010)
15. Raptis, M., Sigal, L.: Poselet key-framing: a model for human activity recognition. In: Proceedings Conference on Computer Vision and Pattern Recognition (CVPR), pp. 2650–2657 (2013)
16. Ryoo, M.S.: Human activity prediction: early recognition of ongoing activities from streaming videos. In: Proceedings IEEE International Conference on Computer Vision (ICCV), pp. 1036–1043 (2011)
17. Ryoo, M.S., Aggarwal, J.K.: UT-Interaction Dataset, ICPR contest on semantic description of human activities (SDHA) (2010). http://cvrc.ece.utexas.edu/SDHA2010
18. Ryoo, M.S., Aggarwal, J.K.: Stochastic representation and recognition of high-level group activities. Int. J. Comput. Vis. (IJCV) **93**(2), 183–200 (2011)
19. Schuldt, C., Laptev, I., Caputo, B.: Recognizing human actions: a local SVM approach. In: Proceedings International Conference on Pattern Recognition (ICPR), pp. 32–36 (2004)
20. Sefidgar, Y.S., Vahdat, A., Se, S., Mori, G.: Discriminative key-component models for interaction detection and recognition. Comput. Vis. Image Underst. (CVIU) **135**, 16–30 (2015)
21. Sener, F., İkizler-Cinbis, N.: Two-person interaction recognition via spatial multiple instance embedding. J. Vis. Commun. Image Represent. **32**(C), 63–73 (2015)
22. Supancic III, J.S., Ramanan, D.: Self-paced learning for long-term tracking. In: Proceedings Conference on Computer Vision and Pattern Recognition (CVPR), pp. 2379–2386 (2013)
23. Tian, Y., Sukthankar, R., Shah, M.: Spatiotemporal deformable part models for action detection. In: Proceedings Conference on Computer Vision and Pattern Recognition (CVPR), pp. 2642–2649 (2013)
24. van Gemeren, C., Tan, R.T., Poppe, R., Veltkamp, R.C.: Dyadic interaction detection from pose and flow. In: Proceedings Human Behavior Understanding Workshop (ECCV-HBU), pp. 101–115 (2014)
25. van Gemert, J.C., Jain, M., Gati, E., Snoek, C.G.M.: APT: action localization proposals from dense trajectories. In: Proceedings British Machine Vision Conference (BMVC), p. A117 (2015)
26. Wang, H., Kläser, A., Schmid, C., Cheng-Lin, L.: Dense trajectories and motion boundary descriptors for action recognition. Int. J. Comput. Vis. (IJCV) **103**(1), 60–79 (2013)
27. Weinzaepfel, P., Revaud, J., Harchaoui, Z., Schmid, C.: DeepFlow: large displacement optical flow with deep matching. In: Proceedings IEEE International Conference on Computer Vision (ICCV), pp. 1385–1392 (2013)
28. Yang, Y., Baker, S., Kannan, A., Ramanan, D.: Recognizing proxemics in personal photos. In: Proceedings Conference on Computer Vision and Pattern Recognition (CVPR), pp. 3522–3529 (2012)
29. Yang, Y., Ramanan, D.: Articulated human detection with flexible mixtures of parts. IEEE Trans. Pattern Anal. Mach. Intell. (PAMI) **35**(12), 2878–2890 (2013)
30. Yao, B., Nie, B., Liu, Z., Zhu, S.-C.: Animated pose templates for modelling and detecting human actions. IEEE Trans. Pattern Anal. Mach. Intell. (PAMI) **36**(3), 436–452 (2014)

31. Yun, K., Honorio, J., Chattopadhyay, D., Berg, T.L., Samaras, D.: Two-person interaction detection using body-pose features and multiple instance learning. In: Proceedings Conference on Computer Vision and Pattern Recognition Workshops (CVPRW), pp. 28–35 (2012)
32. Zhang, Y., Liu, X., Chang, M.-C., Ge, W., Chen, T.: Spatio-temporal phrases for activity recognition. In: Fitzgibbon, A., Lazebnik, S., Perona, P., Sato, Y., Schmid, C. (eds.) ECCV 2012. LNCS, vol. 7574, pp. 707–721. Springer, Heidelberg (2012). doi:10.1007/978-3-642-33712-3_51

Vision Based Applications

Convoy Detection in Crowded Surveillance Videos

Zeyd Boukhers[1(✉)], Yicong Wang[2], Kimiaki Shirahama[1], Kuniaki Uehara[2], and Marcin Grzegorzek[1]

[1] Research Group for Pattern Recognition, University of Siegen, Siegen, Germany
{zeyd.boukhers,kimiaki.shirahama,marcin.grzegorzek}@uni-siegen.de
[2] Graduate School of System Informatics, Kobe University, Kobe, Japan
wang@ai.cs.kobe-u.ac.jp, uehara@kobe-u.ac.jp

Abstract. This paper proposes detection of *convoys* in a crowded surveillance video. A convoy is defined as a group of pedestrians who are moving or standing together for a certain period of time. To detect such convoys, we firstly address pedestrian detection in a crowded scene, where small regions of pedestrians and their strong occlusions render usual object detection methods ineffective. Thus, we develop a method that detects pedestrian regions by clustering feature points based on their spatial characteristics. Then, positional transitions of pedestrian regions are analysed by our convoy detection method that consists of the clustering and intersection processes. The former finds groups of pedestrians in one frame by flexibly handling their relative spatial positions, and the latter refines groups into convoys by considering their temporal consistences over multiple frames. The experimental results on a challenging dataset shows the effectiveness of our convoy detection method.

Keywords: Crowded video surveillance · Group activities · Convoy detection · Pedestrian detection in crowded scenes

1 Introduction

Automatic analysis of crowded surveillance videos has recently drawn research attention. Especially, detection of group activities is an important issue since they are fraught with valuable information which can portend many unusual activities. Most existing works use flow to detect group activities by considering a group pattern as a set of moving feature points [13], other methods tackle stationary groups which are also represented as a batch of feature points [20]. However, in crowd environments, people move in all directions which makes the result complicated. Thus, the existing methods cannot give a substantial addition to analyse people activities. Compared to this, we detect pedestrians in every frame and keep their identities over the frame sequence. Then, we propose to detect one type of group activities called *convoy patterns*, which can gather two or more pedestrians moving or standing together as one pattern.

© Springer International Publishing AG 2016
M. Chetouani et al. (Eds.): HBU 2016, LNCS 9997, pp. 137–147, 2016.
DOI: 10.1007/978-3-319-46843-3_9

We propose to detect and track objects in a crowded scene, which is not easy regarding the human detection, because pedestrians are occluded by each other and their ROIs are very small to be detected. In addition, the high number of targets makes the tracking very complex in terms of pedestrian's visual appearance, position prediction and time consumption. Our method clusters feature points detected in every frame based on corner detection in order to form objects, where we consider an object as a set of feature points sharing the same spatial characteristics.

Contrary to most methods which study people's group activities by considering multi-patterns (e.g., Uniform, Stable, Conflict, etc.) [13], we focus only on detection of convoys. This is because the multitude of patterns provides confusing outputs, since the difference between properties is intangible and difficult to be definable. Moreover, this pattern diversity does not have high contribution in order to understand people group activities. The difficulty of detecting convoys lies in the high pedestrian density, where patterns change their intra properties (e.g., relative positions of pedestrians in one group) and inter properties (e.g., a group can cross another group) over time. Therefore, we implement a two-phase algorithm which consists of a density clustering phase and an intersection phase, where the former is unaffected to the intra properties of pedestrians. In other words, even if the relative positions of pedestrians in a group changed, it allows them to stay in the same group as long as they are densely connected. Meanwhile, we handle the inter properties by intersecting pedestrian groups iteratively, where if the same pedestrians continuously form a group over a frame sequence, they are regarded as a convoy.

2   Related Work

Detecting and estimating crowd motion patterns have been largely used [12,17, 21] to model and understand pedestrian interactions. Using the same approach another study addresses the problem of studying normal crowd behaviours [15] (e.g., bottlenecks, lanes and blocking) and abnormal ones [8,9] by considering psychological and physical effects.

Recently, researchers considered group activities as an important cue to understand and analyse crowded scenes. For example, Shao *et al.* [13] use motion pattern estimation in order to detect, characterise and quantify group properties (e.g., Uniformity, Conflict, etc) in a crowded scene. This method is based on identifying an anchor tracklet for every group, which can be selected based on its continuous existence in the scene. Thus, several further frames need to be processed and therefore the method cannot run sequentially (online). Many other methods analyse mobile social groups based on relative distances and velocities of moving pedestrians [1,2,4,7] but they ignore stationary crowd groups.

On the other hand, other studies demonstrate the high impact of stationary groups on changing traffic properties of crowded and no-crowded scenes [10,18–20]. In [10,19], researchers consider that stationary groups have much influence on the walking path of other moving pedestrians, as opposed to moving groups which can influence the velocities of other moving pedestrians. Moreover, Yi *et al.* [18,20] show the impact of stationary groups on the travel time of a pedestrian from his/her entrance to the scene until his/her exit.

In this paper, we propose a sequential method to detect and track small groups (convoys), where our method does not require further frame processing, which lets it be more suitable for real scenarios. We identify all pedestrians in order to reduce the density of detection, where one-pedestrian groups are neglected. In addition, convoys extracted by our method are general in the sense that they cover both moving and stationary groups of pedestrians. Hence, we do not have to prepare a model for each type of group like the existing methods [13].

3   Method

Our method consists of two parts, *Human detection and tracking* and *Convoy detection*, which are explained below.

3.1   Human Detection and Tracking

We target a static surveillance camera displaying a wide view, where tracks of many pedestrians are captured for long durations. For such a video, most object detection methods have restrictions regarding image resolution, object deformation, lighting condition, occlusion and computational complexity. We therefore present a new method to detect objects by clustering feature points as it can be seen in Fig. 1. We explain in the following the clustering method of the first frame by applying corner and edge detection methods in order to determine object ROIs from the background. Furthermore, we explain the clustering improvement on further frames, where feature point tracking is used as a new clustering criterion.

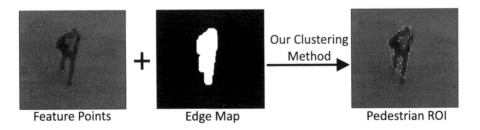

| Feature Points | Edge Map | Pedestrian ROI |

Fig. 1. An overview of pedestrian detection.

Clustering on the First Frame: We invest in the idea that the existence of objects such as pedestrians in an image causes a discontinuity in the spatial characteristics, which allows the distinction of objects from the background. We detect *Features from Accelerated Segment Test (FAST)* [11] which is a fast corner detection method and outputs a set of feature points. In addition, the complete pedestrian's ROI is assumed to be traced by a closed boundary or inside a bigger closed boundary. Edge detection is a good cue to show the details of the image and delineate objects. Let c be a set of extracted feature points $\mathbf{k} = \{k_1, k_2, ..., k_n\}$ of the image I and M be its Canny edge map. We then cluster the set of feature points using the following Algorithm 1.

Algorithm 1. Clustering algorithm (k)

---

1 **while** $\mathbf{k}^* \neq \emptyset$ **do**
2 | Select an anchor a^i point from $\mathbf{k}^*$ to form new cluster $\mathbf{c}^i$;
3 | $\mathbf{k}^* = \mathbf{k}^* \setminus a^i$;
4 | Select from $\mathbf{k}^*$ a set of feature points $\mathbf{b}^i$ satisfying clustering criteria;
5 | **if** $\mathbf{b}^i \neq \emptyset$ **then**
6 | | Assign $\mathbf{b}^i$ to $\mathbf{c}^i$;
7 | | $\mathbf{k}^* = \mathbf{k}^* \setminus \mathbf{b}^i$;

Here, $\mathbf{k}^*$ denotes a set of non-clustered points, and the anchor point is determined based on the number of its neighbours and their average distance. More specifically, the anchor point has the highest number of neighbours with the lowest average distance, where it is the center of the ellipse neighbourhood. To complete the cluster, we assign other points to a^i, these points must be inside the same closed edge. This is illustrated in Fig. 1 where feature points inside the region of the human in the edge map are merged into a cluster. In addition, the height and width of the cluster should be less or equal to α and β, which are pre-defined values of the maximum object height and width, respectively.

Clustering Improvement on a Frame Sequence: For further frames in the sequence, we have another cue to improve the clustering and eliminate non-pedestrian clusters. Using a fixed camera permits the distinction between stationary and moving pixels, where stationary pixels represent the background and moving pixels represent moving and stationary pedestrians, since people cannot avoid moving locally in the small region they occupy, even if they are stationary. We therefore consider only feature points which appear in I_t and I_{t-1}, and propose to neglect feature points which cannot be tracked. Using the open source library VLFeat [16], we extract a set of keypoints $\mathbf{s} = \{s_1, s_2, .., s_{n'}\}$ for the image I_t. Since a huge number of SIFT keypoints can be extracted covering the whole image, the final set of feature points of I_t is $\mathbf{l} = \mathbf{k} \cap \mathbf{s}$. Let $\mathbf{l}°$ be the final feature points of I_{t-1}. The new characterisation of feature points $\mathbf{l}$ is the move properties (Velocity and Direction) from $\mathbf{l}°$, which is done by finding the closest point descriptors in I_t to those in I_{t-1}, that is measured by the L2 norm of the difference between them [16]. As a result, we can obtain a set of feature points that are likely to characterise moving and stationary pedestrians in the scene.

Afterwards, the same steps of Algorithm 1 are used in order to cluster the set of features $\mathbf{l}$ into pedestrian regions. We also consider a new characterisation to assign feature points to the cluster formed by an anchor point, where points of one cluster must have the same velocity and direction. Note that clusters with a velocity $\simeq 0$ are neglected.

3.2   From Trajectories to Convoys

We explain our method to extract convoy patterns from trajectories detected by the above-mentioned method. Our idea is similar to previous papers [5,6], but we propose a new pattern called *noncontinuous convoy*. We first introduce the definition of convoy, the clustering and intersection method for convoy detection. Then, we extend it to the detection of noncontinuous convoys.

Noncontinuous Convoy: Jeung *et al.* [5] proposed a convoy as a group of objects which are *density-connected* with each other during a consecutive period of time. Here, *density-connected* is a measurable way of determining whether people stay together or not spatially. However, convoys with such density-connected objects are not as capable as expected in real-life circumstances because of the very rigid constraint of consecutiveness. For example, two pedestrians who are walking together may not be density-connected for a few seconds for some reasons. Furthermore, pedestrian detection may be unstable, or two pedestrians may become separated by an obstacle, etc. Therefore, they are not considered as density-connected, so we cannot represent the trajectories of pedestrians walking together properly.

Thus, we propose a noncontinuous convoy which is a convoy pattern defined by relaxing the constraint of consecutiveness. For the previous example, as long as cluster members (pedestrians) do not go separate for a long time, the convoy formed by them does not end, that is, it persists until they get back together. To quantify the tolerable length of separation, we adopt a parameter called *elasticity*, which is the minimal ratio of the number of density-connected frames to the length of a noncontinuous convoy. We can say that a convoy is equivalent to a noncontinuous convoy of 1.0 *elasticity*. Meanwhile, a noncontinuous convoy of 0.5 elasticity means that convoy members are density-connected in more than half of the convoy length.

Clustering and Intersection: We implement a two-phase algorithm. It consists of a clustering phase and an intersection phase to extract convoys from trajectories. For intuition, Fig. 2 represents an example case of 4 pedestrians. At the beginning, candidates are found as clusters of pedestrians who are spatially close to each other at each time moment [3]. As time goes by, candidates are separated due to the intersection with candidates from the previous frame. Once the duration of candidates becomes longer than the duration threshold, it is detected as a convoy. In Fig. 2, a candidate denoted as '$(p_0, p_1), 2$' means that p_0 and p_1 are density-connected since 2 frames ago. A candidate is the intersection result of clusters in the current frame and candidates in the previous frame. A candidate exceeding the duration threshold in italic font is output as

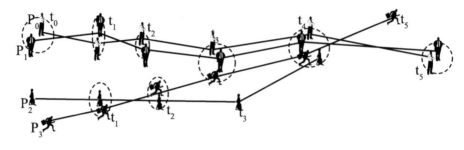

	t_0	t_1	t_2	t_3	t_4	t_5
Clusters	(p_0, p_1)	(p_0, p_1) (p_2, p_3)	(p_0, p_1) (p_2, p_3)	(p_0, p_1, p_3)	(p_0, p_1, p_2, p_3)	(p_0, p_1)
Candidates	(p_0, p_1), 1	(p_0, p_1), 2 (p_2, p_3), 1	(p_0, p_1), 3 (p_2, p_3), 2	(p_0, p_1), 4 (p_0, p_1, p_3), 1	(p_0, p_1), 5 (p_0, p_1, p_3), 2 (p_0, p_1, p_2, p_3), 1	(p_0, p_1), 6
Convoy			(p_0, p_1), 3	(p_0, p_1), 4	(p_0, p_1), 5	(p_0, p_1), 6

Fig. 2. An illustration of convoy detection.

a convoy. Note that in this example a convoy involves at least two persons and its minimum duration is set to 2 frames.

Candidate Expiring Mechanism: We propose a candidate expiring mechanism in order to detect noncontinuous convoys. The key idea is to avoid flushing the candidate set so that convoys whose sizes are smaller than the threshold are not removed immediately. Specifically, besides the existing *duration* attribute, we add a *createdTime* attribute to each candidate in order to count the length of a noncontinuous convoy. Thus, at any moment, we know how many frames have passed since a particular candidate was created by calculating *currentTime − createdTime*. Meanwhile, the unmodified *duration* is the number of frames where they are density-connected. So, we can remove a candidate if it satisfies:

$$\frac{duration}{currentTime - createdTime} \leq elasticity \tag{1}$$

Algorithm 2 shows a pseudo code of the clustering and intersection algorithm with the candidate expiring mechanism, where it first performs a density-based clustering algorithm DBSCAN [3] for all the pedestrians in the coming frame (line 1–3). The output of DBSCAN are clusters of density-connected pedestrians. Then, for initialisation, if there are no candidates, the current clusters are added to the candidate set R and continue to process the next frame (line 4–7). Then the algorithm refines convoy candidates by intersecting them with the new clusters

---

Algorithm 2. Clustering and Intersection

Data: cluster size threshold m, duration threshold k, DBSCAN distance threshold e,
          DBSCAN density threshold u and sequenced trajectory data frame$S$
Result: convoys that reached the thresholds

```
1  for frame s in S do
2  |    initialize empty set R';
3  |    cluster the objects in s with respect to e and u;
4  |    if R = ∅ then
5  |    |    for cluster c in s do
6  |    |    |    add c to R;
7  |    |    continue;
8  |    for cluster r in R do
9  |    |    for cluster c in s do
10 |    |    |    new candidate r' = r ∩ c;
11 |    |    |    duration(r') = duration(r) + duration(s);
12 |    |    |    if size(r') ≥ m then
13 |    |    |    |    createdTime(r') = currentTime;
14 |    |    |    |    add r' to R';
15 |    |    |    add c to R';
16 |    add R' to R;
17 |    for cluster r in R do
18 |    |    if duration(r) ≥ k then
19 |    |    |    output r as a qualified convoy;
20 |    |    if duration(r)/(currentTime − createdTime(r)) ≤ l then
21 |    |    |    remove r from R;
```

(line 8–11). An intersection result that exceeds the size threshold (in our case, the number of pedestrians must be more than 2) is stored as a new candidate (line 12–14). Then, the new clusters are added to R (line 15). R is updated for the next frame (line 16). Then, the algorithm begins to evaluate the candidates by elasticity. If a candidate exceeds the duration threshold, it is output as a convoy (line 17–19). Meanwhile, a candidate is discarded if it does not satisfy the elasticity criteria (line 20–21).

4 Experiment and Result

In this chapter, we evaluate our convoy detection method on the pedestrian walking path dataset [19], which is of one hour length and contains more than 12.000 pedestrians moving in all directions. Figure 3a shows an example result of our pedestrian detection, where (*)s denote the ground truth of pedestrian positions provided by [19], and boundaries represent the output of our method. In addition, Fig. 3b shows an example of noncontinuous convoy detection, where trajectories are obtained by firstly detecting human regions in consecutive frames, and analysing temporal transitions of those regions' positions using Algorithm 2. As a result, transitions that are close to each other in the time dimension are regarded as convoys, and depicted by coloured lines in Fig. 3b. For more detailed results, readers can see a demonstration video on http://youtu.be/p4zN39u_Waw.

| Pedestrian Detection | Convoy Detection |

Fig. 3. Left: an example of pedestrian detection (a), Right: an example of noncontinuous convoy detection (b).

4.1 Evaluation of Pedestrian Detection

Convoy detection lies on the accuracy of pedestrian tracking which is related to the accuracy of pedestrian detection. Our human detection method is controlled by several parameters, such as the size of a pedestrian ROI, and the minimum number of feature points to form a pedestrian. Table 1 shows the result of our method with 4 different parameter combinations for 600 frames ($\simeq$6 min). Due to the small size of pedestrian projections into the image plan, a pedestrian detection is correct only if the annotated point is surrounded by our output boundary, which can be seen in Fig. 3a. Here, *LFT*, *HFT*, *SZT* and *BZT* represent low feature point number threshold, high feature point number threshold, small pedestrian size threshold and big pedestrian size threshold respectively. Then, for each parameter combination, we compute the precision and recall based on the above-mentioned criteria. For example, in the case of *LFT-BZT* which will be used in the following experiments, among 697 pedestrians existing in the scene, 596 are correctly detected and 164 falsely detected. Therefore, the result in Table 1 shows the effectiveness of our clustering method to localise objects in the crowded scene.

Table 1. Pedestrian detection result using 4 different parameter combinations.

	LFT - SZT	HFT - SZT	LFT - BZT	HFT - BZT
Recall	0.97	0.9	0.86	0.79
Precision	0.7	0.74	0.78	0.86

4.2 Evaluation of Convoy Detection

Table 2 shows the result of our convoy detection method on the same sequence using the parameter combination of human detection which provides the

Table 2. Convoy detection result.

	S1	S2	S3
Recall	0.88	0.97	0.97
Precision	0.47	0.47	0.92

median result. For fair evaluation, the following three cases are considered: The first is 'S1' where the result of convoy detection is compared to the ground truth defined manually. In the second case 'S2', our result is compared to a subclass of the ground truth, where we neglect convoys whose members fail to be detected by our pedestrian detection method. The evaluation of the last case 'S3' is done by neglecting detected convoys which are formed by *false positive pedestrian detection (FPPD)*.

Overall, Table 2 shows the effectiveness of our convoy detection method. Especially, as shown in 'S3', when all pedestrians are detected and well tracked, where it is able to detect almost all convoys. The high recall in 'S2' indicates that even when pedestrian false negatives are considered, the performance of convoy detection is acceptable. In other words, although our method outputs many false positive convoys, only a few true positive convoys are missed. This is desirable for security surveillance. Meanwhile, convoy detection is very sensitive to pedestrian false positives as it can be seen for the precisions in 'S1' and 'S2', but by neglecting pedestrian false positives, the precision of convoy detection becomes extremely better as indicated by the precision in 'S3'.

The continuity of a convoy is very important for group activity analysis. For each detected convoys, the beginning and the end are manually annotated. Figure 4a represents the interruption histogram which shows the frequency of interruption number per convoy. We conclude that more than 50 % of detected convoys are not interrupted and even for interrupted convoys, the number of interruptions is low compared to the length of convoys in such a crowded scene, where the longest convoy in the ground truth appears in 156 frames ($\simeq$1,8 min). This indicates the effectiveness of detecting non-continuous convoys, even though very few convoys are interrupted because of pedestrian detection failure.

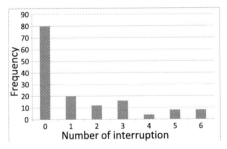 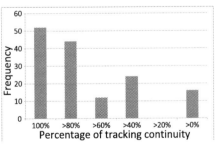

Fig. 4. Left: interruption histogram (a), Right: tracking continuity histogram (b).

We also evaluate the temporal coverage of each extracted convoy, compared to its actual temporal existence in the ground truth. The histogram which can be seen in Fig. 4b shows the frequency of convoy completeness, where about 65 % of detected convoys are tracked for more than 80 % of their existence, where from 148 annotated convoys, 52 ($\simeq$35 %) are completely detected and tracked for their whole existences and if we tolerate missing 20 % of a convoy's temporal existence, we find that 96 ($\simeq$65 %) convoys are tracked.

5   Conclusion

In this paper, a new method of convoy detection in crowded scenes is proposed. The method is followed by a concrete evaluation and detailed experiment. In our current implementation, although convoy detection is carried out online, the extraction and matching of feature points is slow. Thus, we seek in the future to use GPU for solving this problem [14]. Also, we believe that the method can be improved by using feedback mechanism between pedestrian detection and convoy detection in order to reduce false positive detection.

Acknowledgments. The research work by Zeyd Boukhers leading to this article has been funded by the German Academic Exchange Service (DAAD). Research and development activities in this article have been in part supported by the German Federal Ministry of Education and Research within the project "Cognitive Village: Adaptively Learning Technical Support System for Elderly" (Grant Number: 16SV7223K).

References

1. Amer, M.R., Todorovic, S.: A chains model for localizing participants of group activities in videos. In: Proceedings of ICCV 2011, pp. 786–793 (2011)
2. Chang, M.C., Krahnstoever, N., Ge, W.: Probabilistic group-level motion analysis and scenario recognition. In: Proceedings of ICCV 2011, pp. 747–754 (2011)
3. Ester, M., Kriegel, H.-P., Sander, J., Xu, X.: A density-based algorithm for discovering clusters in large spatial databases with noise. In: Proceedings of KDD 1996, pp. 226–231 (1996)
4. Ge, W., Collins, R.T., Ruback, R.B.: Vision-based analysis of small groups in pedestrian crowds. IEEE Trans. Pattern Anal. Mach. Intell. **34**(5), 1003–1016 (2012)
5. Jeung, H., Shen, H.T., Zhou, X.: Convoy queries in spatio-temporal databases. In: Proceedings of ICDE 2008, pp. 1457–1459 (2008)
6. Jeung, H., Yiu, M.L., Zhou, X., Jensen, C.S., Shen, H.T.: Discovery of convoys in trajectory databases. Proc. VLDB Endowment **1**(1), 1068–1080 (2008)
7. Lan, T., Wang, Y., Yang, W., Robinovitch, S.N., Mori, G.: Discriminative latent models for recognizing contextual group activities. IEEE Trans. Pattern Anal. Mach. Intell. **34**(8), 1549–1562 (2012)
8. Mahadevan, V., Li, W., Bhalodia, V., Vasconcelos, N.: Anomaly detection in crowded scenes. In: Proceedings of CVPR 2010, pp. 1975–1981 (2010)
9. Mehran, R., Oyama, A., Shah, M.: Abnormal crowd behavior detection using social force model. In: Proceedings of CVPR 2009, pp. 935–942 (2009)

10. Moussaid, M., Perozo, N., Garnier, S., Helbing, D., Theraulaz, G.: The walking behaviour of pedestrian social groups and its impact on crowd dynamics. PLoS ONE **5**(4), 1–7 (2010)
11. Rosten, E., Drummond, T.: Machine learning for high-speed corner detection. In: Leonardis, A., Bischof, H., Pinz, A. (eds.) ECCV 2006. LNCS, vol. 3951, pp. 430–443. Springer, Heidelberg (2006). doi:10.1007/11744023_34
12. Shao, J., Kang, K., Loy, C.C., Wang, X.: Deeply learned attributes for crowded scene understanding. In: Proceedings of CVPR 2015, pp. 4657–4666 (2015)
13. Shao, J., Loy, C.C., Wang, X.: Scene-independent group profiling in crowd. In: Proceedings of CVPR 2014, pp. 2227–2234 (2014)
14. Sinha, S.N., Frahm, J.-M., Pollefeys, M., Genc, Y.: Feature tracking and matching in video using programmable graphics hardware. Mach. Vis. Appl. **22**(1), 207–217 (2011)
15. Solmaz, B., Moore, B.E., Shah, M.: Identifying behaviors in crowd scenes using stability analysis for dynamical systems. IEEE Trans. Pattern Anal. Mach. Intell. **34**(10), 2064–2070 (2012)
16. Vedaldi, A., Fulkerson, B.: VLFeat: an open and portable library of computer vision algorithms (2008). http://www.vlfeat.org/. Accessed 21 Apr 2016
17. Wang, X., Ma, X., Grimson, W.E.L.: Unsupervised activity perception in crowded and complicated scenes using hierarchical Bayesian models. IEEE Trans. Pattern Anal. Mach. Intell. **31**(3), 539–555 (2009)
18. Yi, S., Li, H., Wang, X.: Pedestrian travel time estimation in crowded scenes. In: Proceedings of ICCV 2015, pp. 3137–3145 (2015)
19. Yi, S., Li, H., Wang, X.: Understanding pedestrian behaviors from stationary crowd groups. In: Proceedings of CVPR 2015, pp. 3488–3496 (2015)
20. Yi, S., Wang, X., Lu, C., Jia, J.: L0 regularized stationary time estimation for crowd group analysis. In: Proceedings of CVPR 2014, pp. 2219–2226 (2014)
21. Zhou, B., Wang, X., Tang, X.: Understanding collective crowd behaviors: learning a mixture model of dynamic pedestrian-agents. In: Proceedings of CVPR 2012, pp. 2871–2878 (2012)

First Impressions - Predicting User Personality from Twitter Profile Images

Abhinav Dhall[(✉)] and Jesse Hoey

David R. Cheriton School of Computer Science,
University of Waterloo, Waterloo, Canada
{abhinav.dhall,jesse.hoey}@uwaterloo.ca

Abstract. This paper proposes a computer vision based pipeline for inferring the perceived personality of users from their Twitter profile images. We humans make impressions on a daily basis during communication. The perception of personality of a person gives information about the person's behaviour and is an important attribute in developing rapport. The personality assessment in this paper is referred to as *first impressions*, which is similar to how humans create a mental image of another person by just looking at their profile pictures. In the proposed automated pipeline, hand crafted (engineered) and learnt feature descriptors are computed on user profile images. The effect of image background is assessed on the perception of the personality from a profile picture. A multivariate regression approach is used to predict the big five personality traits - *agreeableness, conscientiousness, extraversion, openness* and *neuroticism*. We study the correlation between the big five personality traits generated from Tweet analysis with the proposed profile image based framework. The experiments show high correlation for scene based *first impressions* perception. It is interesting to note that the results generated by analysing a profile image uploaded by a user in a particular point in time are in sync with the *first impression* traits generated by investigating Tweets posted over a longer duration of time.

Keywords: Personality perception · Big five personality traits · Profile images · Scene descriptors

1 Introduction

First impression is the perception formed by an individual on an initial encounter with another person. The perception of a person plays an important role in human-human and human-machine interactions. From the perspective of human-centric systems inferring the personality of a user can result in the personalisation of services [1]. It is argued that a user's personality effects their behaviour online [2]. In this paper, we investigate the perceived personality of Twitter user based on their profile pictures (Sample pictures in the study - Fig. 1).

Automatic analysis of human behavior perception is a non-trivial task. Similar to earlier works [2–6] we have used the personality traits described by the

© Springer International Publishing AG 2016
M. Chetouani et al. (Eds.): HBU 2016, LNCS 9997, pp. 148–158, 2016.
DOI: 10.1007/978-3-319-46843-3_10

Fig. 1. Sample profile picture images used in this study.

Big Five (BF) [7] personality model. The BF model is widely used in psychology, to analyse human personality. The BF model broadly divides the human perception into the five following dimensions [8]:

- *agreeableness* - tendency for compliance and cooperation;
- *conscientiousness* - tendency to planned behavior and have orderliness;
- *extraversion* - how outgoing or shy a person is;
- *neuroticism* - feeling negative emotions such as anxiety, hostility etc.;
- *openness* - ease in adopting new ideas and experiences.

In an interesting study, Rojas et al. [9] evaluate geometric and texture facial descriptors for predicting the face based personality traits. The geometric descriptors encoded the spatial structure and the texture descriptors represent a face at holistic level. The facial data used in the experiments was collected in the lab by recording students.

Celiktutan et al. [10] present a multimodal technique for inferring the BF traits in the continuous time domain. Facial movement statistics and texture features are extracted from aligned faces and Mel-frequency cepstral coefficients are computed over the audio signal. The experiments are performed on the MAP-TRAITS challenge database [11]. The MAPTRAITS challenge consisted of two sub-challenges: continuous frame-level personality trait inference and video based personality assessment. Kaya et al. [12] proposed a continuous multimodal BF prediction model during the MAPTRAITS challenge based on canonical correlation analysis and extreme learning machine based regression.

Continuous frame-level BF traits inference is important from the perspective of personalising human-machine interaction. We argue that early personality assessment, a so-called *first impression* of personality, is essential in assistive technology machines. Let us take the example of an assistive technology framework like a handwashing system for persons with Alzheimer's disease [13]. Given the fluctuating and uncertain personality profile of a person with Alzheimer's, a *first impression* assessment for initialising the type of prompts is considered important. Over the course of the use of the hand washing system, the personality can be assessed at frequent intervals to generate the correct prompt. Todorov et al. [14] argue that the *first impression* perception based on the face analysis of a person can vary with different photos. In the study they observe that the ratings vary w.r.t. context.

For e.g.: a picture of the same person for an online dating profile vs political campaign can generate different ratings. Furthermore, presence of facial features such as moustaches also make a difference in the perception of the *first impression* personality ratings. In the context of the hand washing assistive framework as the personality of a person with dementia varies, bootstrapping the system with the *first impression* is thought to be potentially very useful.

Joshi et al. [8] analysed the personality of a subject during human-virtual agent interaction (SEMAINE database [15]) under different situational context. Along with the BF labels, likeability and engagement were also studied. In order to remove the noisy labels from the crowd-sourced labels, the contribution of the a particular labeller whose ratings have larger deviation from the mean is down weighted. The authors found that the perception of the traits of attractiveness and likeability do not change much with a different situational context.

Biel et al. [16] analysed YouTube videos ('video blogs') using universal facial expression labels as high-level features computed frame-wise. Ferwerda et al. [17] conducted an interested study on Instagram images to predict a user's personality. Image descriptor statistics are extracted from the Hue Saturation Value color space. Furthermore, attributes such as the number of faces in the images posted by a user and number of full bodies in the images. Facial features are also computed and HOG feature is extracted. They also study the effect of filters on the perception of personality. Celli et al. [18] proposed a study to analyse Facebook user personality from their profile picture. SIFT feature is extracted from interest points and dimensionality reduction is applied using singular vector decomposition.

In this paper, we propose a pipeline for inferring the perceived personality of users from their profile image. In the next section the hand crafted and the learnt features are discussed, followed by the experimental analysis.

2   Pipeline

Given the varied nature of images, we chose the Mixture of Pictorial Structures (MoPS) face and fiducial points detection [19]. MoPS is the current state-of-art method for face, facial parts location and head pose detection. It consists of two models: an appearance model and a shape model. The appearance model is a set of HOG based part detectors and the shape model applies a tree structure to the part detector response. Post computation of the facial parts location of an input, affine warp is applied to transform the face into a canonical frame.

2.1   Facial Descriptors

The Pyramid of Histogram of Gradients (PHOG) [20] is an extensively used descriptor in computer vision. It is a scale robust extension of the popular HOG descriptor. The descriptor is computed by applying the Canny edge detector followed by dividing an image into non-overlapping block. Further, a Sobel operator is applied to compute the orientation directions, which are further binned into a histogram. We call PHOG based approach as *Face_PHOG*. PHOG has been successfully used in face based emotion recognition [21] along with the Local Phase Quantisation (LPQ) descriptor [22]. LPQ is a local binary pattern descriptor, which is robust to blur and illumination. Given the nature of the images on social networking platforms, LPQ has proved to be an effective descriptor. LPQ is computed by applying short Fourier transform on an image. The coefficients are then analysed using a LBP operator. We refer to the LPQ based pipeline as Face_LPQ.

Along with the hand crafted features (PHOG and LPQ), we also extract learning based features. Recently, a deep learning based convolutional nearest neighbor model - VGG-Very-Deep-16 [23] has been successfully applied to the problem of face recognition. The model has been trained on 900,000 images taken from the internet. We extracted fc_7 layer based feature as an input for learning a regression model. The model is applied on aligned faces and referred to as Face_VGG.

2.2   Scene Descriptor

Along with the face information, the background, body parts may also affect the perception of personality of a subject. The Instagram study [17] analyse color statistics as one way of measuring the scene. We explicitly compute a robust scene descriptor - CENsus TRansform hISTogram (CENTRIST) [24]. CENTRIST is computed by applying the so-called Census transform operator, which is similar to LBP. The CENTRIST descriptor captures the statistics of the background (or the scene) at a holistic level. In order to encode the spatial structure of an image, CENTRIST is computed on non-overlapping blocks. We compute Principal Component Analysis (PCA) on the normalised block-wise CENTRIST descriptors and call it Scene_CENTRIST. Similar to the face based CNN features, we extract CNN based features from a deep model trained on the Image Net data. The model [25] is trained for classifying 1000 categories. The feature of convolutional layer fc_7 are extracted and referred to as Scene_ImageNet.

2.3   Big Five Traits Prediction

For inferring the BF traits, we train a Kernel Partial Least Square (KPLS) regression model [26]. The mapping function $\mathcal{F}$ is learnt using the Kernel Partial Least Squares (KPLS) [26] regression framework. The partial least square based algorithms have recently become very popular in computer vision [27–29]. PLS has been used for dimensionality reduction [28,29]. For face analysis [30] use KPLS based regression for simultaneous dimensionality reduction and predicting happiness intensity. The training set $\mathbf{X}$ is a set of input samples x_i of dimension N. Here x_i is the facial or scene level descriptor. $\mathbf{Y}$ is the corresponding set of BF traits vectors y_i of dimension $M = 5$. Then for a given test sample matrix X_{test} the estimated labels matrix $\hat{Y}$ is given by:

$$\hat{\mathbf{Y}} = \mathbf{K}_{test}\mathbf{R} \tag{1}$$

$$\mathbf{R} = \mathbf{U}(\mathbf{T}^T\mathbf{K}^T\mathbf{U})^{-1}\mathbf{T}^T\mathbf{Y} \tag{2}$$

where $\mathbf{K}_{test} = \mathbf{\Phi_{test}}\mathbf{\Phi}^T$ is the kernel matrix for test samples X_{test}. $\mathbf{T}$ and $\mathbf{U}$ are the $n \times p$ score matrices of the p extracted latent projections. For more details and the derivation of KPLS regression technique, see [26].

3   Data

The images used in the experiment are Twitter profile pictures collected by [31]. They also recorded upto 3200 recent tweets of each user. The baseline BF ratings [31] are created by analysing the tweets of the users. Park et al. [32] text analysis model is used to generate the BF ratings. Their experimental results with a high Pearson correlation score of r > .3 shows the effectiveness of their model. The ratings are further mean normalised to 0 [31]. The trait wise ranges are as follows: *agreeableness*: $[-2.2{:}4.3]$, *conscientiousness*: $[-3.5{:}4.3]$, *extraversion*: $[-3.7{:}2.7]$, *openness*: $[-3.2{:}2.4]$ and *neuroticism*: $[-4.6{:}2.6]$. The profile images are taken from 26533 users based on operational account and profile image containing face. Sample images in the experiment can be seen in Fig. 1. In the next section it is observed that profile image based *first impression* has high correlation with the values generated from analysing Tweets. It is important to note that the Tweets (upto 3200) have been posted over a longer duration of time by a user and we can infer the traits with in reasonable accuracy (w.r.t. Tweets based inference) by analysing the profile picture of a user.

4   Experiments

Given the varied nature (different face sizes, frontal/profile face, occlusion & illumination) of the profile images on Twitter, we use three MoPS models[1]. The three face models (*face_99*, *face_149* & *face_1050*) are applied in a cascade approach. The models differ on the basis of number of facial part detectors. Based on the facial parts locations, affine warp is computed to transform the face into a canonical frame. For computing the PHOG descriptor[2] the parameters were chosen empirically as follows: bin size = 8; angle = [0–360] & pyramid levels = 3. The rotation invariant version of LPQ[3] is computed with default parameters. Similarly for the CENTRIST descriptor, publicly available implementation[4] is used. The pre-trained VGG models (imagenet-vgg-m-2048 and vgg-face) are part of the MatConvNet toolkit[5].

We also tried normalising Face_VGG and Scene_ImageNet by dividing the vector with its sum and name them Face_VGGNorm and Scene_ImageNetNorm, respectively. Normalisation is performed within the PHOG and CENTRIST descriptors as well. For analysing the performance of the techniques, we used

---

[1] http://www.cs.cmu.edu/~deva/papers/face/index.html.
[2] http://www.robots.ox.ac.uk/~vgg/research/caltech/phog.html.
[3] http://www.cse.oulu.fi/CMV/Downloads/LPQMatlab.
[4] https://github.com/sometimesfood/spact-matlab.
[5] http://www.vlfeat.org/matconvnet.

Table 1. The table shows the RMSE based comparison of the different descriptors. Here the ground truth are the trait values generated by analysing upto 3200 Tweets of a user. The correlation between the profile and Tweets based inference is mentioned in the round brackets. Values in the bold represent the lowest RMSE. ope - openness, con. - conscientiousness, ext. - extraversion, agr. -agreeableness & neu. - neuroticism.

Feature	ope.	con.	ext.	agr.	neu.	avg.
Face_PHOG	0.40 (0.06)	**0.39** (0.23)	0.43 (0.11)	0.35 (0.16)	0.35 (0.16)	**0.38**
Face_VGG	0.53 (0.00)	0.43 (0.00)	0.43 (0.01)	0.39 (0.01)	0.51 (−0.01)	0.46
Face_VGGNorm	**0.39** (0.20)	**0.37** (0.36)	0.42 (0.21)	**0.34** (0.23)	**0.34** (0.26)	**0.37**
Face_LPQ	0.44 (0.00)	0.43 (0.00)	0.43 (0.00)	0.35 (0.00)	0.39 (0.00)	0.41
Scene_CENTRIST	0.40 (0.05)	0.40 (0.05)	0.42 (0.05)	0.35 (0.08)	0.35 (0.07)	0.39
Scene_ImageNet	0.55 (0.02)	0.44 (−0.04)	0.45 (−0.06)	0.39 (0.05)	0.50 (0.00)	0.47
Scene_ImageNetNorm	0.40 (0.01)	0.41 (−0.02)	0.43 (0.01)	0.35 (0.01)	0.35 (0.01)	0.39

Root Mean Square Error (RMSE) metric. We also compute the correlation between the BF dimensions (*first impressions*) generated from profile image and the BF traits generated from Tweets analysis. The number of basis for KPLS was set as 5, empirically. 18000 samples were used for training the model.

Table 1 shows the performance of the proposed techniques. It is interesting to note that for the *openness* trait, Face_VGGNorm, Face_PHOG and scene descriptors (Scene_CENTRIST and Face_VGG) perform better than Face_VGG and Scene_ImageNet. Post normalisation of Scene_ImageNet, the error decreases significantly and is on par with Face_PHOG. Face_VGGNorm performs the best out of all, similar superior performance was observed in the original paper for the task of face recognition [23]. We observe particularly high correlation for *openness* between Tweets based analysis and the scene descriptors (Scene_CENTRIST, Scene_ImageNetNorm).

Furthermore, *openness* can also be described as imaginativeness ability and acceptance to new ideas, it is plausible that the interesting locations/backgrounds, where the picture is clicked loosely relate to a person's ability to explore new places. This can be one reason why scene descriptors works well for this trait in particular. In Fig. 3, the second half (High) of the bottom row has subjects posing with outdoor and art-like backgrounds. It is interesting to note that in the same figure, images with low *openness* also have outdoor backgrounds. However, their faces are not clear/frontal.

For the *conscientiousness* trait, face structure seems to play an important role. This also encompasses the facial expression. Liu et al. also observed similar findings, when they analysed positive expressions and *conscientiousness*. Face_VGGNorm performs the best, similar to the case of *openness*. Face_VGGNorm also has a high correlation ($r > .2$) with the Tweet based *conscientiousness* trait inference. Figures 2 and 3, subjects with high *conscientiousness* score show smiling expressions and have close to frontal face pose. Again, similar to *openness* the normalisation of Scene_ImageNet increases the performance in the case of *conscientiousness* trait inference. On performing correlation analysis between the tweet generated

Fig. 2. Sample outputs (low and high BF intensity) inferred from the Face_PHOG approach.

Fig. 3. Sample outputs (low and high BF intensity) inferred from the Scene_ImageNetNorm approach.

[31] and Face_VGGNorm based generated BF traits, we found high correlation for *conscientiousness*. This can also mean that the first impression (for *conscientiousness*) generated from a profile picture is similar to long term personality analysis (Tweets).

The performance of the hand crafted and the learnt features is almost similar for the *extraversion* trait with the Scene_CENTRIST descriptor performing slightly better than others. For *agreeableness* trait, the RMSE performance for Face_PHOG, Face_LPQ and two CENTRIST, normalised Scene_CENTRIST are same. It is to be noticed that for computing a scene level descriptor, no face detection and alignment is required. If face detection fails, not much can be done with the face descriptors. Therefore, it is plausible that scene level descriptors are more appropriate for the *agreeableness* trait. Similar pattern of performance is seen in the results of the *neuroticism* trait. The correlation is high for Face_VGGNorm, Face_PHOG, Scene_CENTRIST with Tweets analysis for *agreeableness* and *neuroticism*.

5   Conclusion and Future Work

In this paper, we propose a pipeline for detecting user personality from their Twitter profile pictures. Face-only and holistic-level scene analysis are studied for their suitability in predicting the big five personality traits. For inferring the traits, kernel partial least square regression is used. The experiments are conducted on profile images downloaded from Twitter. The experiments give an interesting insight into the applicability of scene-level descriptors for analysing the personality of a user. It is interesting to note that with a holistic scene descriptor like CENTRIST captures the *first impression*, which is highly correlated with the BF generated from Tweets analysis. Further, CNN based learnt feature combined with KPLS regression performs the best as compared to handcrafted features (PHOG, LPQ & CENTRIST). We observe that CNN based scene features have low RMSE and high correlation for trait such as *openness*.

In this study, individual features are used to train the KPLS regression. A future scope of the work is to explore various fusion techniques, specially the ones suitable for scene and face features. Another possibility is to compute high-level attributes such as facial action units and facial features (beard, glasses etc.) and use them as features along with the low-level feature descriptors used in this paper. It will also be interesting to explore the use of structured regression methods such as twin Gaussian process regression and structured support vector regression for infer the personality traits. Retraining the CNN models with the end goal of BF trait assessment can also improve the performance of the framework. The long term aim of this work is to integrate automatic *first impression* assessment in an assistive technology system (such as the handwashing framework [13]). We hypothesise that getting the *first impression* correct, when a person first starts using such an assistive technology, is crucial for generating effective prompts and for ensuring uptake of the technology. Further proceeding in this direction, the proposed methods will be experimented on profile images of elderly people.

Acknowledgments. This work was supported by AGE-WELL NCE Inc., a member of the Networks of Centres of Excellence program and Alzheimer's Association grant ETAC-14-321494.

References

1. Ferwerda, B., Schedl, M., Tkalcic, M.: Personality & emotional states: understanding users music listening needs. In: UMAP 2015 Extended Proceedings (2015)
2. Lepri, B., Staiano, J., Rigato, G., Kalimeri, K., Finnerty, A., Pianesi, F., Sebe, N., Pentland, A.: The sociometric badges corpus: a multilevel behavioral dataset for social behavior in complex organizations. In: 2012 International Conference on Privacy, Security, Risk and Trust (PASSAT), pp. 623–628. IEEE (2012)
3. Mairesse, F., Walker, M.: Automatic recognition of personality in conversation. In: Proceedings of the Human Language Technology Conference of the NAACL, Companion Volume: Short Papers, pp. 85–88. Association for Computational Linguistics (2006)
4. Mohammadi, G., Vinciarelli, A.: Automatic personality perception: prediction of trait attribution based on prosodic features. IEEE Trans. Affect. Comput. **3**, 273–284 (2012)
5. Pianesi, F., Mana, N., Cappelletti, A., Lepri, B., Zancanaro, M.: Multimodal recognition of personality traits in social interactions. In: Proceedings of the 10th International Conference on Multimodal Interfaces, pp. 53–60. ACM (2008)
6. Camastra, F., Vinciarelli, A.: Automatic personality perception. In: Camastra, F., Vinciarelli, A. (eds.) Machine Learning for Audio, Image and Video Analysis. Advanced Information and Knowledge Processing, pp. 485–498. Springer, London (2015)
7. John, O.P., Srivastava, S.: The Big Five trait taxonomy: History, measurement, and theoretical perspectives. Handb. Pers. Theory Res. **2**(1999), 102–138 (1999)
8. Joshi, J., Gunes, H., Goecke, R.: Automatic prediction of perceived traits using visual cues under varied situational context. In: ICPR, pp. 2855–2860 (2014)
9. Rojas, M., Masip, D., Todorov, A., Vitria, J.: Automatic prediction of facial trait judgments: appearance vs. structural models. PLoS ONE **6**(8), e23323 (2011)
10. Celiktutan, O., Gunes, H.: Automatic prediction of impressions in time and across varying context: personality, attractiveness and likeability. IEEE Trans. Affect. Comput. (2016)
11. Celiktutan, O., Eyben, F., Sariyanidi, E., Gunes, H., Schuller, B.: MAPTRAITS 2014: the first audio/visual mapping personality traits challenge. In: Proceedings of the 2014 Workshop on Mapping Personality Traits Challenge and Workshop, pp. 3–9. ACM (2014)
12. Kaya, H., Salah, A.A.: Continuous mapping of personality traits: a novel challenge and failure conditions. In: Proceedings of the 2014 Workshop on Mapping Personality Traits Challenge and Workshop, pp. 17–24. ACM (2014)
13. Lin, L., Czarnuch, S., Malhotra, A., Yu, L., Schröder, T., Hoey, J.: Affectively aligned cognitive assistance using Bayesian affect control theory. In: Pecchia, L., Chen, L.L., Nugent, C., Bravo, J. (eds.) IWAAL 2014. LNCS, vol. 8868, pp. 279–287. Springer, Heidelberg (2014). doi:10.1007/978-3-319-13105-4_41
14. Todorov, A., Porter, J.M.: Misleading first impressions different for different facial images of the same person. Psychol. Sci. **25**(7), 1404–1417 (2014)

15. McKeown, G., Valstar, M., Cowie, R., Pantic, M., Schroder, M.: The SEMAINE database: annotated multimodal records of emotionally colored conversations between a person and a limited agent. IEEE Trans. Affect. Comput. **3**(1), 5–17 (2012)
16. Biel, J.I., Gatica-Perez, D.: The YouTube lens: crowdsourced personality impressions and audiovisual analysis of vlogs. IEEE Trans. Multimedia **15**(1), 41–55 (2013)
17. Ferwerda, B., Schedl, M., Tkalcic, M.: Using Instagram picture features to predict users' personality. In: Tian, Q., Sebe, N., Qi, G.-J., Huet, B., Hong, R., Liu, X. (eds.) MMM 2016. LNCS, vol. 9516, pp. 850–861. Springer, Heidelberg (2016). doi:10.1007/978-3-319-27671-7_71
18. Celli, F., Bruni, E., Lepri, B.: Automatic personality and interaction style recognition from Facebook profile pictures. In: Proceedings of the 22nd ACM international conference on Multimedia, pp. 1101–1104. ACM (2014)
19. Zhu, X., Ramanan, D.: Face detection, pose estimation, and landmark localization in the wild. In: Proceedings of the IEEE Conference on Computer Vision and Pattern Recognition (CVPR), pp. 2879–2886 (2012)
20. Bosch, A., Zisserman, A., Munoz, X.: Representing shape with a spatial pyramid kernel. In: Proceedings of the ACM international conference on Image and video retrieval (CIVR), pp. 401–408 (2007)
21. Dhall, A., Asthana, A., Goecke, R., Gedeon, T.: Emotion recognition using PHOG and LPQ features. In: Proceedings of the IEEE Conference Automatic Faces and Gesture Recognition workshop FERA, pp. 878–883 (2011)
22. Ojansivu, V., Heikkilä, J.: Blur insensitive texture classification using local phase quantization. In: Elmoataz, A., Lezoray, O., Nouboud, F., Mammass, D. (eds.) ICISP 2008. LNCS, vol. 5099, pp. 236–243. Springer, Heidelberg (2008). doi:10.1007/978-3-540-69905-7_27
23. Parkhi, O.M., Vedaldi, A., Zisserman, A.: Deep face recognition. In: British Machine Vision Conference, vol. 1, p. 6 (2015)
24. Wu, J., Rehg, J.M.: CENTRIST: a visual descriptor for scene categorization. IEEE Trans. Pattern Anal. Mach. Intell. **33**(8), 1489–1501 (2011)
25. Chatfield, K., Simonyan, K., Vedaldi, A., Zisserman, A.: Return of the devil in the details: delving deep into convolutional nets. arXiv preprint arXiv:1405.3531 (2014)
26. Rosipal, R.: Nonlinear partial least squares: an overview. In: Chemoinformatics and Advanced Machine Learning Perspectives: Complex Computational Methods and Collaborative Techniques. ACCM, IGI Global (2011)
27. Guo, G., Mu, G.: Simultaneous dimensionality reduction and human age estimation via kernel partial least squares regression. In: Proceedings of the IEEE Conference on Computer Vision and Pattern Recognition (CVPR), pp. 657–664 (2011)
28. Schwartz, W.R., Kembhavi, A., Harwood, D., Davis, L.S.: Human detection using partial least squares analysis. In: Proceedings of the IEEE International Conference on Computer Vision (ICCV), pp. 24–31 (2009)
29. Schwartz, W.R., Guo, H., Davis, L.S.: A robust and scalable approach to face identification. In: Daniilidis, K., Maragos, P., Paragios, N. (eds.) ECCV 2010, Part VI. LNCS, vol. 6316, pp. 476–489. Springer, Heidelberg (2010). doi:10.1007/978-3-642-15567-3_35
30. Dhall, A., Joshi, J., Radwan, I., Goecke, R.: Finding happiest moments in a social context. In: Lee, K.M., Matsushita, Y., Rehg, J.M., Hu, Z. (eds.) ACCV 2012, Part II. LNCS, vol. 7725, pp. 613–626. Springer, Heidelberg (2013). doi:10.1007/978-3-642-37444-9_48

31. Liu, L., Preotiuc-Pietro, D., Samani, Z.R., Moghaddam, M.E., Ungar, L.: Analyzing personality through social media profile picture choice. In: Tenth International AAAI Conference on Web and Social Media (2016)
32. Park, G., Schwartz, H.A., Eichstaedt, J.C., Kern, M.L., Kosinski, M., Stillwell, D.J., Ungar, L.H., Seligman, M.E.: Automatic personality assessment through social media language. J. Pers. Soc. Psychol. **108**(6), 934 (2015)

Author Index

Printed in the United States
By Bookmasters